CAMBRIDGE SCHOOL

Chaucer

THE
General Prologue
TO THE CANTERBURY TALES

Edited by David Kirkham and Valerie Allen

CAMBRIDGE
UNIVERSITY PRESS

The publishers would like to thank Professor Helen Cooper for her help in the preparation of this edition.

PUBLISHED BY THE PRESS SYNDICATE OF THE UNIVERSITY OF CAMBRIDGE
The Pitt Building, Trumpington Street, Cambridge, United Kingdom

CAMBRIDGE UNIVERSITY PRESS
The Edinburgh Building, Cambridge CB2 2RU, UK
40 West 20th Street, New York, NY 10011–4211, USA
10 Stamford Road, Oakleigh, VIC 3166, Australia
Ruiz de Alarcón 13, 28014 Madrid, Spain
Dock House, The Waterfront, Cape Town 8001, South Africa

http://www.cambridge.org

First published 1999
Third printing 2001

Printed in the United Kingdom at the University Press, Cambridge

Typeface Garamond (*Adobe*) 11/12.5 pt and 12.5/14.5 pt   *System* QuarkXPress®

A catalogue record for this book is available from the British Library

ISBN 0 521 59588 8 paperback

Prepared for publication by Elizabeth Paren
Designed and formatted by Geoffrey Wadsley
Illustrated by Peter Edwards
Picture research by Valerie Mulcahy

Thanks are due to the following for permission to reproduce photographs:
John Bethell Photography, pages 36, 44; E. T. Archive/Royal Library Escorial, Spain, page 49;
The Fotomas Index, pages 32, 46; Hulton Getty Picture Collection, pages 6, 19, 21, 22, 25,
58, 71, 88/89, 91; Image Bank/Paulo Magalhaes, page 30; Mansell/Time Inc./Katz, page 40

For cover photograph: Thomas Lydgate and Pilgrims leaving Canterbury from Prologue to
Canterbury Tales 1516, E. T. Archive/British Library Roy18DIIf.148

Contents

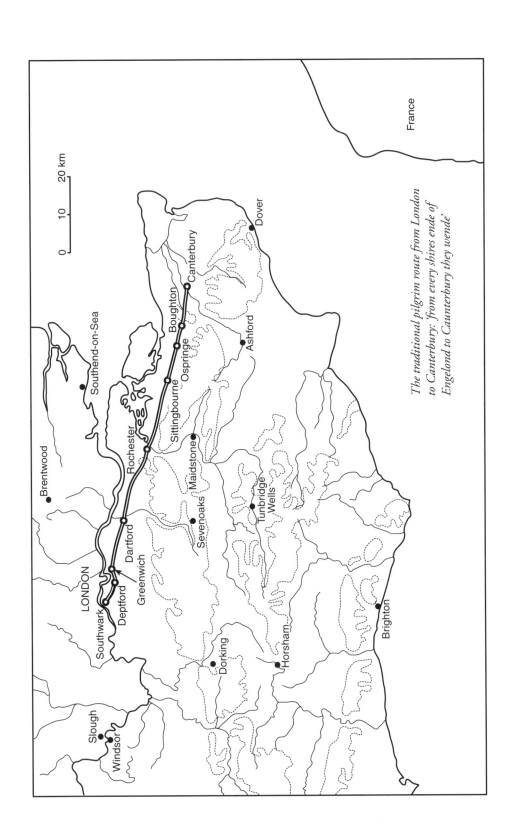

The traditional pilgrim route from London to Canterbury: 'from every shires ende of Engelond to Caunterbury they wende'

Introduction

The first encounter with a page of Chaucer in its original form can be a disconcerting experience. Initially, few words look familiar. Even when the meaning has been puzzled out, the reader is faced with an account of people who lived and died in a world very different from our own. The fourteenth century seems very far away, and you might be forgiven for thinking that *The Canterbury Tales* are 'too difficult'.

The aim of this series is, therefore, to introduce you to the world of Chaucer in a way that will make medieval language and life as accessible as possible. With this in mind, we have adopted a layout in which each right-hand page of text is headed by a brief summary of content, and faced by a left-hand page offering a glossary of more difficult words and phrases as well as commentary notes dealing with style, characterisation and other relevant information. There are illustrations, and suggestions for ways in which you might become involved in the text to help make it come alive.

If the initial hurdles are lowered in this way, Chaucer's wit and irony, his ability to suggest character and caricature, and his delight in raising provocative and challenging issues from various standpoints, can be readily appreciated and enjoyed. There is something peculiarly delightful in discovering that someone who lived six hundred years ago had a sense of humour and a grasp of personalities and relationships as fresh and relevant today as it was then.

Each tale provides material for fruitful discussion of fourteenth century attitudes and modern parallels. It is important to realise that the views expressed by the teller of any one tale are not necessarily Chaucer's own. Many of the activities suggested are intended to make you aware of the multiplicity of voices and attitudes in *The Canterbury Tales*. A considerable part of the enjoyment of the tales comes from our awareness of the tongue-in-cheek presence of the author, who allows his characters to speak for themselves, thereby revealing their weaknesses and obsessions.

Essential information contained in each book includes a brief explanation of what *The Canterbury Tales* are, followed by some hints on handling the language. There is then a brief introduction to the teller of the relevant story, his or her portrait from the General Prologue, and an initial investigation into the techniques Chaucer uses to present characters.

The left-hand page commentaries give information applicable to the text. Finally, each book offers a full list of pilgrims, further information on Chaucer's own life and works, some background history, and greater discussion of specific medieval issues. Suggestions for essays and themes to be explored are also included. On page 96 there is a relatively short glossary of the words most frequently encountered in the text, to supplement the more detailed glossary on each page.

Chaucer's tales are witty, clever and approachable, and raise interesting parallels with life today. His manipulation of the short story form is masterly. We hope this edition brings *The Canterbury Tales* alive and allows you to appreciate Chaucer's art with ease and enjoyment.

What are The Canterbury Tales?

They are a collection of stories, loosely linked together, apparently told by a variety of storytellers with very different characters and from different social classes. In fact, both the storytellers and the tales are the creation of one man, Geoffrey Chaucer. Chaucer imagines a group of pilgrims, setting off from the Tabard Inn one spring day on the long journey from London to the shrine of St Thomas à Becket in Canterbury – a journey that on horseback would take about four days.

To make time pass more pleasantly the pilgrims agree to tell stories to one another. Chaucer begins by introducing his pilgrims to the reader, in descriptions which do much to reveal the characters, vices and virtues of each individual. We learn more from the way each person introduces his or her tale, still more from the tales themselves and the way in which each one is told, and even further information is offered by the manner in which some pilgrims react to what others have to say. By this means Chaucer provides a witty, penetrating insight into the attitudes, weaknesses, virtues and preoccupations of English men and women of the fourteenth century. Some of their behaviour and interests may seem very strange to modern readers; at other times they seem just like us.

CHAUCER'S VIEW OF THE PILGRIMS

Chaucer's view of his pilgrims is often complex, although characters such as the Knight, the Parson and the Ploughman are clear examples of deep virtue, without reservations of any kind. Some characters, for example the Prioress, are shown as having weaknesses that they themselves do not realise. The Friar is an example of a deeply corrupt man who is very affable to those from whom he makes his living. Other characters are described straightforwardly as unattractive physically (the Miller) or morally (the Shipman).

Chaucer uses several 'voices' in The General Prologue (and throughout all the Tales that follow it). The first is his own, in that every word is the work of Chaucer

The destination of the pilgrims – Canterbury Cathedral today

the poet. Secondly comes the voice of Chaucer the narrator or pilgrim. He puts himself among the pilgrims – indeed he tells two stories later on – and makes some direct and indirect judgments on the characters he is describing. At times he makes himself seem almost a simpleton in this voice, but at other times he can be blunt or subtly ironical about the characters he is describing.

Chaucer's third voice can be heard when he speaks through one of his characters. There is a good deal of talk – often fiercely quarrelsome – during and between the telling of the Tales in the main body of the work, but in The General Prologue we hear Harry Bailey, the landlord of the Tabard Inn, speaking with confidence and authority to the pilgrims, not worrying about the shyness of the Clerk or the Prioress, organising them and (later in the work) keeping the peace very effectively. What he says to and about the pilgrims is firm and downright, and contrasts with the subtlety, artlessness, irony and diffidence of Chaucer the narrator.

A fourth voice is more a structure than a voice, but it has a similar effect. The world of Chaucer's time was firmly structured, socially, religiously and morally. How people were supposed to live, in theory at least, was generally known. Any departure from this ideal was therefore obvious to people of the time. This difference, between life as it was supposed to be lived and as it was lived in practice, gave Chaucer a framework, a device of great flexibility: he could describe his characters, relate their actions and words, and his listeners would draw appropriate conclusions about the difference between the ideal and the actual. The Knight, the Parson and the Ploughman are presented as ideals and are to some extent a point of comparison against which other characters may be judged.

The fourth voice is heard in the changes in society that are described by Chaucer. The Prioress and the Monk, for instance, are, in their different ways, rather surprising people. Where we might expect an unworldly spirituality we see people self-consciously engaged with the world. They seem to see no contradiction between their vows and their enjoyment of the good things of life; they are not monsters of evil, but they are out of their cloisters and there is not much poverty about their way of life. To what extent can we see them as typical?

Other clerical characters are more clearly at fault. The Pardoner and Summoner are corrupt, using their functions within the church to make a good living from poor believers. Yet they do seem aware of their badness; indeed they boast of what they do. But how far are they aware of any implicit judgement on them? To what extent might the apparent tolerance of their faults arise from a weary acceptance of widespread corruption of this sort?

Some of the lay characters are similarly not ideal. The Franklin is a wealthy man with no idea that his pleasant, self-indulgent life might be seen as less than perfect. He is what he is, and he does what he does; questions of how he might, or should, live do not seem to arise. The Merchant, for all his expensive clothes and brave talk, is in debt; the Sergeant of the Law is an able but slippery man, ready to turn his skills to account for his clients and for himself. The ideal lives alongside the real in this work, but the judgement is left for the readers to make, if they have eyes to see.

7

Chaucer's language

The unfamiliar appearance of a page of Chaucerian English often prevents students from pursuing their investigations any further. It does no good to hear people telling them that this man used language with a complexity and subtlety not found in any writer of English anywhere before him. They remain unimpressed. He looks incomprehensible.

In fact, with a little help, it does not take very long to master Chaucer's language. Much of the vocabulary is the same, or at least very similar to, words we use today. On page 96 there is a glossary of the unfamiliar words most frequently used in this text, and these will quickly become familiar. Other words and phrases that could cause difficulties are explained on the pages facing the actual text.

The language of Chaucer is known as Middle English – a term covering English as it was written and spoken in the period roughly between 1150 and 1500. It is difficult to be more precise than this, for Middle English itself was changing and developing throughout that period towards 'modern' English.

Old English (Anglo-Saxon) was spoken and written until around 1066, the time of the Norman Conquest. This event put power and authority in England into the hands of the Norman lords, who spoke their own brand of Norman French. Inevitably this became the language of the upper classes. The effect was felt in the church, for speedily the control of the monasteries and nunneries throughout the land was given to members of the new French-speaking aristocracy. Since these religious houses were the seats of learning and centres of literacy, the effect on language was considerable. If you were a wealthy Anglo-Saxon, eager to get on in the world of your new over-lords, you learnt French. Many people were bi- or even trilingual: French was the language of the law courts and much international commerce; Latin was the language of learning (from elementary school to the highest levels of scholarship) and of the church (from the parish church services to the great international institution of the papacy).

Gradually, as inter-marriage between Norman French and English families became more common, the distinction between the two groups and the two languages became blurred. Many French words became absorbed into Old English, making it more like the language we speak today. In the thirteenth century King John lost control of his Norman lands, and as hostility between England and France grew, a sense of English nationalism strengthened. In 1362 the English language was used for the first time in an English parliament. At the same time, Geoffrey Chaucer, a young ex-prisoner of the war against the French, was sharpening his pens and his wit, testing the potential for amusement, satire and beauty in this rich, infinitely variable, complex literary tool.

Although some Tales are partly, or entirely, in prose, *The Canterbury Tales* are written largely in rhyming iambic couplets. This form of regular metre and rhyme is flexible enough to allow Chaucer to write in a range of styles. He uses the couplet form to imitate colloquial speech as easily as philosophical debate. Most importantly, Chaucer wrote poetry 'for the ear'; it is written for the listener, as much as for the reader. Rhyme and alliteration add emphasis and link ideas and objects together in a way that is satisfying for the audience. The words jog along as easily and comfortably as the imaginary pilgrims and their horses jogged to Canterbury.

PRONUNCIATION

Chaucer spoke the language of London, of the king's court, but he was well aware of differences in dialect and vocabulary in other parts of the country. In the Reeve's Tale, for instance, he mocks the north country accents of the two students. It is clear, therefore, that there were differences in pronunciation in the fourteenth century, just as there are today.

Having been told that Chaucer wrote verse to be read aloud, students may be dismayed to find that they do not know how it should sound. There are two encouraging things to bear in mind. The first is that although scholars feel fairly sure they know something about how Middle English sounded, they cannot be certain, and a number of different readings can still be heard. The second concerns the strong metrical and rhyming structure Chaucer employed in the writing of his Tales.

Finding the rhythm Follow the rhythm of the verse (iambic pentameter), sounding or omitting the final 'e' syllable in the word as seems most appropriate. In the line

And yet he hadde a thumbe of gold, pardee.

it would add an unnecessary syllable if the final 'e' in 'hadde' and 'thumbe' were to be pronounced. An 'e' at the end of a word almost always disappears if it is followed by a vowel or a word beginning with 'h'.

In the case of these examples:

As leene was his hors as is a rake,

and

His table dormant in his halle alway –

the best swing to the regular 10-syllabled line is achieved by sounding the 'e' (as a neutral vowel sound, like the 'u' in put, or the 'a' in about) in the words 'leene', 'table' and 'rake', but not in 'halle'.

Other points In words beginning with the letter 'y' (for example 'ywet', 'yknowe') the 'y' is sounded as it would be in the modern 'party'. Many consonants now silent were pronounced – as in 'knight', 'wrong'. All the consonants would be given voice in words such as 'neigheboures' and 'knight' and the 'gh' would be sounded like the Scots 'ch' in 'loch'. The combination 'ow' (for example 'yow', meaning 'you') is pronounced as 'how', and the 'ei' in 'streit' would be like the 'a' sound in 'pay'.

For more ideas of what the language might have sounded like, listen to the tapes of Chaucer published by Cambridge University Press and by the 'Chaucer Man' (Trevor Eaton).

WARM-UP ACTIVITIES

- Choose a long, self-contained section from the text: lines 19–42 of The General Prologue are a useful example. After a brief explanation of the content, if considered necessary, students work in pairs, speaking alternately, and changing over at each punctuation point. It should be possible to develop a fair turn of speed without losing the sense of the passage.

- Again in pairs, choose about 10 lines of text; as one of the pair maintains a steady beat [^/^/^/^/^/] the partner does his or her best to fit the words to the rhythm.
- Choose a long self-contained unit from the text. Students walk round the room, speaking the script, and turning left or right at each punctuation mark. An alternative to this might be to use one 'speaker' to four or five 'listeners', representing Chaucer's audience. Each time the speaker reaches a punctuation mark he/she should switch to a new member of the audience, who should respond by looking alert and animated, only allowed to sink back into apathy when he/she moves to the next one.

GRAMMATICAL POINTS

Emphatic negatives Whereas a person who stated that he 'wasn't going nowhere, not never' might be considered grammatically incorrect nowadays, Chaucer uses double or triple negatives quite often, to give a statement powerful added emphasis. One of the best known is in his description of the Knight in The General Prologue:

>He never yet no vilenye ne sayde
>In al his life, unto no manner wight.

Another occurs in the Wife of Bath's Prologue:

>...may they nat biquethe for no thing
>To noon of us hir vertuous living.

In both cases the multiple negatives strengthen the force of what is being said.

Word elision In modern written English words and phrases are often run together (elided) to represent the spoken form of these words: 'didn't', 'can't', 'won't', 'I've', and so on. Chaucer uses short forms of words too, especially in forming the negative. In his time it was usual to form a negative by placing 'ne' before the verb. Often this elided into the verb. Thus 'ne was' is the Chaucerian form of 'was not', but it was often written as 'nas'. Elsewhere in The General Prologue Chaucer writes 'noot', short for 'ne woot', meaning 'did not know'.

The 'y' prefix The past tense of a verb sometimes has a 'y' before the rest of the verb, particularly when the verb is passive:

his halve cours yronne	has run half his course
a man is wel yshrive	a man is fully absolved
he sholde ypunisshed be	he should be punished

The 'possessive' form of nouns In modern English we indicate possession by means of an apostrophe: 'the hat of the man' becomes 'the man's hat'. Middle English had a particular formation that is still used in modern German. Where we now use an apostrophe followed by an 's', Chaucer uses the suffix 'es': 'the man's hat' becomes 'the mannes hat', with the 'e' indicating that the word has two syllables.

Introduction to The General Prologue

The work opens with a moving evocation of the world waking up from winter, of life returning, and of people's longings for life and for change. It is this longing – religious and non-religious in origin – that makes people gather for their journey. Before they set out, Chaucer tells us that he is going to describe them as he saw them ('so as it semed to me', line 39). The description of each pilgrim follows, occupying most of The General Prologue.

The Knight is travelling with his son, the Squire, and a servant, the Yeoman, as his retinue. The Knight has just returned from the holy wars on the fringes of Christendom. They are followed by the Prioress, the Monk and the Friar, all members of religious orders.

The Merchant, the Clerk, the Sergeant at Law and the Franklin are professional men. The Haberdasher, the Dyer, the Carpenter, the Weaver and the Tapicer (accompanied by their wives and their Cook) are a group of skilled and prosperous guildsmen with social ambitions. The Shipman is a rather sinister figure, set apart, as perhaps befits a seafarer. The Doctor is next, but he fits in socially with the Merchant and the Franklin.

The Wife of Bath is a glorious exception to every rule and category. She is followed by the Parson and his brother, the Ploughman, both of them examples of deep Christian goodness. They are followed by: the Miller – a coarse and unpleasant man; the Manciple – an enigmatic domestic bursar for one of the inns of court; the Reeve, who manages his master's estates; the Summoner – a repulsive lecher who uses his position to satisfy his lusts; and the Pardoner – an ambiguous creature who preys upon people's fears of damnation to make a good living for himself.

Chaucer declares that he is describing these characters because it is 'acordaunt to resoun' (line 37). The General Prologue is evidently to be more than a literary amusement; it is also to be a rational account of the pilgrims, their lives and their motives. Nearly 700 lines later he completes his descriptions. He gives a conventional disclaimer (see page 77) that the blunt or uncouth speech used by some of the characters should not be blamed on him but on the need to tell the story properly. This convention becomes a device behind which he can withdraw as a poet and as narrator. The pilgrims will – apparently – speak for themselves, untroubled by social, moral or ecclesiastical disapproval.

The Host, Harry Bailey, suggests that they tell each other tales during the pilgrimage, and offers a prize for the best one. This device introduces the idea of a game, which further distances the pilgrimage from conventional piety. The rules of this game are Chaucer's own. He can use them to digress from his declared purpose and from the accepted norms of religion, society and literary forms to present his ideas and characters. A detail about one character in The General Prologue contrasts with something said by or about another, and Chaucer the narrator takes a different stance to Chaucer the poet when it suits him. The result is a picture of a group of people whose characteristics, earthy and ideal, express the chaotic individuality of ordinary life.

- Read through the first 18 lines, aloud, in small groups. Do not worry about the pronunciation; just read the words to understand the general meaning. It will help to watch the punctuation.
- In groups of four or five read through lines 1–18, looking for references either to a worldly mood or to a religious mood. Read these lines aloud trying to bring out the different moods. Does Chaucer imply that something is stirring in man's spiritual nature? What sort of journey do these readings suggest?
- In the same groups write your own version of lines 1–18 in one long sentence, trying to imitate Chaucer's tone.

1 **shoures soote** sweet showers

2 **droghte of March** [March is in fact a dry month.]

4 **Of which vertu engendred is the flour** whose power brings flowers into bloom

5 **Zephirus** the west wind [bringing warmth and life-giving rain]

eek also

6 **holt** copse

8 **Ram** the sign of Aries [The sun passes through this sign in spring. It also suggests sexual power. There was a sophisticated knowledge of astrology in Chaucer's time; dates and times were often measured by the system of the zodiac.]

10 **That slepen al the night with open ye** amorousness in spring makes birds [probably nightingales] sing for nights on end

11 **(So priketh hem nature in hir corages)** so nature urges them in their desires

13 **palmeres** pilgrims

14 **ferne halwes** distant shrines [**Halwes** means hallows or saints, as in All Hallows Eve (Hallowe'en) – All Saints Eve.]

kowthe known, familiar

15 **every shires ende** from every part of every county

17 **seke** seek

18 **seeke** sick

Chaucer paints a picture, in one long sentence, of the world waking up to spring: he talks about the season itself, plants, Zephirus the warm west wind, the sun in its progress through the zodiac, and birds, all before he mentions people and their spring-time wish to visit foreign parts on pilgrimage. Finally, he narrows the focus to a particular place, Canterbury, where St Thomas the martyr is buried.

Here biginneth the Book of the Tales of Caunterbury

Whan that Aprill with his shoures soote
The droghte of March hath perced to the roote,
And bathed every veine in swich licour
Of which vertu engendred is the flour;
Whan Zephirus eek with his sweete breeth   5
Inspired hath in every holt and heeth
The tendre croppes, and the yonge sonne
Hath in the Ram his halve cours yronne,
And smale foweles maken melodie,
That slepen al the night with open ye   10
(So priketh hem nature in hir corages);
Thanne longen folk to goon on pilgrimages,
And palmeres for to seken straunge strondes,
To ferne halwes, kowthe in sondry londes;
And specially from every shires ende   15
Of Engelond to Caunterbury they wende,
The hooly blisful martir for to seke,
That hem hath holpen whan that they were seeke.

- Chaucer introduces himself directly as pilgrim into his narrative, for the first of many times. What is his mood as he meets his chance companions? How do you know? List the words and phrases that give you this evidence, and then check your conclusions with a partner.
- Read lines 35–42 carefully, and note Chaucer's motives, his intention and his caution about claiming absolute knowledge.
- Read aloud lines 35–39 several times, in your ordinary pronunciation. Does the reading seem to you to limp, or even trip up at some points? Check your list of points against those of a partner, and discuss what could be altered in your reading to make the verse read evenly.
- Chaucer describes his intentions as 'acordaunt to resoun' (line 37), i.e. rational or logical. What do you think this suggests about his purpose? Is it just to entertain?

19	**bifil** it happened		31	**everichon** every one
21	**wenden** travel		33	**made forward** agreed
22	**corage** spirit		34	**as I you devise** as I shall tell you
25	**sondry** various		35	**nathelees** nevertheless
	by aventure yfalle come together by chance		38	**condicioun** the disposition, character and behaviour
27	**wolden** wanted or intended to [A word with a stronger meaning than its modern descendant 'would'.]		40	**degree** rank or place in society [See the section on page 94.]
28	**wide** roomy, comfortable		41	**array** dress and/or condition
29	**esed atte beste** made very comfortable			

Chaucer arrives at the Tabard Inn, which was in Southwark, at the southern end of London Bridge. This was the only bridge across the River Thames in the fourteenth century, and was a convenient starting point for any journey southwards from London. He declares his intention of describing the character and rank of each of the 29 fellow pilgrims he finds there. His account of the pilgrims lasts for nearly 700 lines; it is towards the end of The General Prologue that he returns to telling us about setting out on the pilgrimage.

Bifil that in that seson on a day,
In Southwerk at the Tabard as I lay   20
Redy to wenden on my pilgrimage
To Caunterbury with ful devout corage,
At night was come into that hostelrie
Wel nine and twenty in a compaignie,
Of sondry folk, by aventure yfalle   25
In felaweshipe, and pilgrimes were they alle,
That toward Caunterbury wolden ride.
The chambres and the stables weren wide,
And wel we weren esed atte beste.
And shortly, whan the sonne was to reste,   30
So hadde I spoken with hem everichon
That I was of hir felaweshipe anon,
And made forward erly for to rise,
To take oure wey ther as I yow devise.
But natheless, whil I have time and space,   35
Er that I ferther in this tale pace,
Me thinketh it acordaunt to resoun
To telle yow al the condicioun
Of ech of hem, so as it semed me,
And whiche they weren, and of what degree,   40
And eek in what array that they were inne;
And at a knight than wol I first biginne.

- Read aloud the description of the Knight, in lines 43–66, using your own modern pronunciation. Look up any unfamiliar words in the glossary on page 96. You might need to go to a good modern dictionary for the full meaning of some of them, e.g. 'cristendom' or 'hethenesse'.
- If there is a recording available of The General Prologue being read as Chaucer would have pronounced it, listen to the first few lines, and practise imitating the pronunciation.
- Use the glossary and a dictionary to ensure you know the meaning of lines 51–66. Read these lines out, using your own pronunciation. Try imitating a recording, if one is available.
- To what extent would you say the presentation of the Knight is that of an ideal, rather than a particular person?
- As you read the rest of the descriptions, think about how each of the characters matches the professed ideals of their way of life.

43 **worthy** [The word is used straightforwardly here; with some other characters it is used with varying degrees of irony.]

45 **chivalrie** [A complicated term indicating skill in battle combined with respect for the laws and decencies of war.]

46 **trouthe** honesty, perseverance and faithfulness to his calling [His vocation as a knight of God – with a suggestion of keeping a promise.]

honour high respect because of an exalted character

fredom behaviour and speech worthy of his position [noble, generous and liberal]

curteisie gentleness [well-bred manners, unselfishness, concern for others]

[These complex terms sum up the ideal of a knight's behaviour and manners.]

47 **lordes werre** [He owed a duty of service to his overlord, and had to fight when called on. Under the feudal system, everyone had an overlord to whom he could look for protection, and to whom he swore allegiance and to whom he owed both work and a willingness to fight when called upon. In this case the phrase also suggests the Knight is doing God's work, as God is also his lord.]

48 **ferre** further

49 **cristendom** the area where Christianity held sway

hethenesse all other areas apart from Christendom

52 **hadde the bord bigonne** had presided at a dinner or a feast to honour him

53 **aboven alle nacions** above knights from all other nations

54 **reysed** gone on raids

59 **Grete See** the Mediterranean

63 **In listes thries, and ay slain his foo** three times he had fought victoriously as a champion of Christianity in the lists [in formal single combat with Muslim champions] – he had always slain his foe.

The Knight is socially the most senior person present. Dedicated knights were supposed to spend their lives doing God's work in defence of Christianity. This Knight has fought at Alexandria in Egypt, at Satalie and Lyas in modern Turkey, in Lithuania (Lettow) and Russia (Ruce), at Granada and Algeciras in Spain, at Balmarie in Morocco and Tramissene in Algeria. The battles were real and recent, but a single person could hardly have been to all of them. Chaucer wants to show that this Knight's life has been spent heroically and selflessly, fighting in support of his lord and against non-Christians, sometimes even in alliance with other non-Christians, such as the Lord of Palatie (the ruler of Balat, in modern Turkey).

   A Knight ther was, and that a worthy man,
That fro the time that he first bigan
To riden out, he loved chivalrie,   45
Trouthe and honour, fredom and curteisie.
Ful worthy was he in his lordes werre,
And therto hadde he riden, no man ferre,
As wel in cristendom as in hethenesse,
And evere honoured for his worthinesse.   50
At Alisaundre he was whan it was wonne.
Ful ofte time he hadde the bord bigonne
Aboven alle nacions in Pruce;
In Lettow hadde he reysed and in Ruce,
No Cristen man so ofte of his degree.   55
In Gernade at the seege eek hadde he be
Of Algezir, and riden in Belmarie.
At Lyeys was he and at Satalie,
Whan they were wonne; and in the Grete See
At many a noble armee hadde he be.   60
At mortal batailles hadde he been fiftene,
And foughten for oure feith at Tramissene
In listes thries, and ay slain his foo.
This ilke worthy knight hadde been also
Sometime with the Lord of Palatie   65
Again another hethen in Turkie.

- What extra information do lines 67–78 give us about the Knight's character?
- Look again at lines 70–71. There are four negatives in these lines. What effect do they have on Chaucer's assertion about the Knight?
- Read aloud lines 73–78, with a partner or in a small group. What impression do they give you of the Knight's appearance?
- Look back at Chaucer's declaration of intent in lines 38–41. Has he described the Knight in the manner he promised?
- Look carefully at the Knight's manners in dealing with people generally. How do you think these manners reflect his vocation as a knight and his qualities in battle?
- What conclusions can you draw from the state of the Knight's clothing and equipment?

67	**sovereyn prys** great reputation	73	**array** dress
69	**port** bearing, manner	75	**fustian** thick cloth, serviceable rather than rich
70	**He nevere yet no vileynie ne saide** he had never said anything evil or coarse		**gipon** tunic
		76	**bismotered** stained
71	**wight** person		**habergeon** coat of chain mail worn over the tunic
72	**He was a verray, parfit gentil knight** he was a perfect knight and gentleman ['Gentil' suggests the courteous manners and honourable behaviour suited to his rank.]	77	**viage** journey

18

The Knight has joined the pilgrimage immediately after arriving home from action abroad.
The religious and legal dispensation for wartime killing lapsed as soon as battle was over; on
emerging from battle he had to do penance and seek forgiveness.

And everemoore he hadde a sovereyn prys;
And though that he were worthy, he was wys,
And of his port as meeke as is a maide.
He nevere yet no vileynie ne saide   70
In al his lif unto no maner wight.
He was a verray, parfit gentil knight.
But, for to tellen yow of his array,
His hors were goode, but he was nat gay.
Of fustian he wered a gipon   75
Al bismotered with his habergeon,
For he was late ycome from his viage,
And wente for to doon his pilgrimage.

A castle built by Christian Crusaders in the Middle East: 'At many a noble armee hadde he be'

- Read aloud the description of the Squire. Do you notice any difference in the language Chaucer uses here and the language he used to describe the Knight?
- Make a list of everything Chaucer tell us of the Squire's appearance, character and actions and write a paragraph summarising this information. Compare your lists and paragraph with your partner's.
- List the differences between the Squire and his father. How do you account for them?
- The Squire would have been somewhere between 14 and 18 years old. Think about your own appearance, character and actions and then write a paragraph about yourself, using your paragraph about the Squire as your model. Then try to put some of what you have written into lines with Chaucer's rhythms and rhyme.
- A squire's education was demanding, encompassing chivalry, service to those he owed service, singing, dancing, playing a musical instrument, drawing, writing verses, jousting, hunting, hawking, being a master of hawks, horses and hounds. He had to be stable in character, temperate, generous and with a charitable consideration of others. How does this compare with the education of a 'young gentleman' today?

80   **bacheler** a learner or apprentice [A Bachelor of Arts is similarly a lower degree than a Master of Arts.]

81   **lokkes crulle as they were leyd in presse** curly hair, as if it had been artificially curled [by being laid in curling irons]

84   **delivere** agile

85   **chivachie** campaigning on horseback [His campaigns in Flanders, Artois and Picardy (the same general area as the battles of World War I) may have had something to do with Chaucer's own youthful experience of fighting in northern France, during the Hundred Years war with France, 1337-1451.]

87   **as of so litel space** in such a short time

88   **In hope to stonden in his lady grace** in hopes of winning his lady's favour

89   **embrouded was he, as it were a**

meede his clothes were embroidered with meadow flowers [His appearance is shown to be very fashionable, with a short gown and long sleeves – very impractical for his way of life. Such fashions were frowned on among the middle-aged of the time, but were much encouraged by the fashion-conscious King Richard II.]

91   **floytinge** playing the flute

95   **endite** write verses

96   **juste** joust

      purtreye mentally conceive

97   **nightertale** night time

99   **lowely, and servisable** humble and willing to serve

100   **and carf biforn his fader** carved his father's meat [Carving was considered a gentle and civilised art, and was a recognised form of service for the Squire.]

The Squire is an apprentice knight, learning from his father how to prepare himself for knighthood and how to behave in a manner fitting his high status. Chaucer clearly makes him an admirable example of his kind, but he is also a young lover, a singer, a musician, a writer of songs and producer of drawings. He is conscious of fashion and is an ardent wooer of young women. Chaucer emphasises his youthful vigour and freshness, in contrast to the rather sombre preoccupations of his father after a lifetime of hard service. This freshness also contrasts with many of the more worn and cynical pilgrims whose descriptions follow. He is the only one who is 'as fressh as is the month of May'.

    With him ther was his sone, a yong Squier,
A lovyere and a lusty bacheler,   80
With lokkes crulle as they were leyd in presse.
Of twenty yeer of age he was, I gesse.
Of his stature he was of evene lengthe,
And wonderly delivere, and of greet strengthe.
And he hadde been somtime in chivachie   85
In Flaundres, in Artois, and Picardie,
And born him weel, as of so litel space,
In hope to stonden in his lady grace.
Embrouded was he, as it were a meede
Al ful of fresshe floures, white and reede.   90
Singinge he was, or floytinge, al the day;
He was as fressh as is the month of May.
Short was his gowne, with sleves longe and wide.
Wel koude he sitte on hors and faire ride.
He koude songes make and wel endite,   95
Juste and eek daunce, and weel purtreye and write.
So hoote he lovede that by nightertale
He sleep namoore than dooth a nightingale.
Curteis he was, lowely, and servisable,
And carf biforn his fader at the table.   100

'Short was his gowne, with sleves longe and wide'

- The Yeoman is described almost entirely in visual terms. Read his description carefully, noting all the details. Behind the details, what impression do you receive of his appearance and character?

102   **for him liste ride so**   for it pleased him [the Knight] to ride in this way [i.e. with only one servant]

104   **pecok arwes**   arrows with peacock feathers

      kene   sharp

105   **thriftily**   efficiently

106-7   **Wel koude ... with fetheres lowe**   he could look after his equipment properly: the feathers on his arrows did not droop, and would guide the arrows accurately

109   **A not heed**   a round head, shaped like a nut

      visage   face

110   **Of wodecraft wel koude he al the usage**   he knew all the practices of woodcraft

111   **bracer**   wristguard, used when firing an arrow

112   **bokeler**   buckler, shield

114   **harneised**   mounted

115   **a Cristopher**   a medal of St Christopher

      sheene   shiny

116   **bawdrik**   belt

'Of wodecraft wel koude he al the usage'

A Knight usually had a retinue of followers to maintain his position, but Chaucer tells us that this Yeoman is all the retinue the Knight has. A yeoman was a free man. This one is a trusty follower of the Knight during war-time, and a forester at other times. (A forester in those days had more to do with the hunt than with caring for timber.) He is confident and self-reliant. He serves his lord and he serves nature, satisfied with his position and function. He is also an anonymous and idealised type: his weapons are beautifully made and kept, and he is expert in their use; he is entirely at home in the forest, and his medal of St Christopher suggests his faith and his function as a guard. (St Christopher is the patron saint of foresters and travellers.)

A Yeman hadde he and servantz namo
At that time, for him liste ride so,
And he was clad in cote and hood of grene.
A sheef of pecok arwes, bright and kene,
Under his belt he bar ful thriftily,   105
(Wel koude he dresse his takel yemanly:
His arwes drouped noght with fetheres lowe)
And in his hand he baar a mighty bowe.
A not heed hadde he, with a broun visage.
Of wodecraft wel koude he al the usage.   110
Upon his arm he baar a gay bracer,
And by his side a swerd and a bokeler,
And on that oother side a gay daggere
Harneised wel and sharp as point of spere;
A Cristopher on his brest of silver sheene.   115
An horn he bar, the bawdrik was of grene;
A forster was he, soothly, as I gesse.

A Prioress was important – the head of a Priory, which was an offshoot from an Abbey. Strictly speaking, she should not have been out of her convent on a pilgrimage. The descriptions of her table manners show that her convent had not yet heard of the use of forks, which made their first appearance in the royal court just about the time that Chaucer was writing The General Prologue.

- To what extent do you think Chaucer is being ironic here? To what extent do you think the Prioress is 'ful simple and coy' (line 119)?
- Think about the significance of what Chaucer does not say about her in this section, bearing in mind that she is the head of an important religious house.
- Read aloud lines 127–131, then lines 133–136. How would you describe the tone and the fluency of these two sets of lines? What effect is achieved by placing line 132 between them?
- Imagine the Prioress at dinner in the Tabard Inn. In a group take the parts of the Knight, the Squire, the Prioress, her retinue, and various drunks with coarse manners (there are several among the pilgrims). Mice run across the floor, cats leap on the table, and dogs prowl in the hope of food. How would the Prioress and her retinue (almost certainly what we would now call middle class) react to their surroundings? Discuss your ideas in the light of the Prioress's intense self awareness and her apparent readiness to model herself on the ladies in courtly romances.

120	**Seinte Loy** St Eloi [who had a reputation for courtesy, and never swore]		with a poor accent [Stratford is in east London. The convent there was patronised by the aristocracy, but was not quite the most fashionable.]
121	**cleped madame Eglentine** called Eglantine [Meaning wild rose – a fashionable name taken from courtly romance, not from a saint. The rose was Mary's flower, but was also the symbol of sensual love.]	132	**curteisie** courtly good manners
		134	**ferthing** speck
		136	**raughte** reached
		137	**of greet desport** very cheerful, merry
123	**Entuned in hir nose ful semely** sung through her nose most attractively [but not necessarily devoutly]	139–40	**And peyned hire to countrefete cheere/Of court** took pains to imitate courtly manners ['Imitation' further suggests that she does not come from a courtly background.]
124	**faire and fetisly** gracefully and neatly		
125	**After the scole of Stratford atte Bow**	141	**digne** worthy

Chaucer tells us successively of the Prioress's restraint, her name, her singing of divine services, her French, her dainty table manners, her manner towards others and the reason why she adopts it.

Ther was also a Nonne, a Prioresse,
That of hir smiling was ful simple and coy;
Hire gretteste ooth was but by Seinte Loy;   120
And she was cleped madame Eglentine.
Ful weel she soong the service divine,
Entuned in hir nose ful semely,
And Frenssh she spak ful faire and fetisly,
After the scole of Stratford atte Bowe,   125
For Frenssh of Paris was to hire unknowe.
At mete wel ytaught was she with alle:
She leet no morsel from hir lippes falle,
Ne wette hir fingres in hir sauce depe;
Wel koude she carie a morsel and wel kepe   130
That no drope ne fille upon hire brest.
In curteisie was set ful muchel hir lest.
Hir over-lippe wiped she so clene
That in hir coppe ther was no ferthing sene
Of grece, whan she dronken hadde hir draughte.   135
Ful semely after hir mete she raughte.
And sikerly she was of greet desport,
And ful plesaunt, and amiable of port,
And peyned hire to countrefete cheere
Of court, and to been estatlich of manere,   140
And to ben holden digne of reverence.

How would the Prioress react to this scene of drunken revelry?

- Make two lists: one of the Prioress's feminine qualities and one of the signs of her religious vocation.
- What do you think Chaucer is implying in describing the way she feeds her dogs? Is it good or bad?
- What impression is given of ideal beauty and actual appearance in lines 152–6?
- Who is telling us about the Prioress – Chaucer the pilgrim or Chaucer the writer? Do you think the Prioress would be pleased with her description? Do you think Chaucer wants us to admire the Prioress or not?
- How would you summarise the differences between the portraits given of the Prioress and the Knight?

147 **wastel-breed** fine white bread

149 **smoot it with a yerde smerte** hit it painfully with a stick

150 **conscience** both tender-heartedness and awareness of guilt

151 **wimpul** nun's head dress

pinched pleated [High foreheads in women were much admired, and hair was plucked to widen them further. Nuns' foreheads were covered by their wimples, except when, as here, the nun wore a pleated wimple to show off her forehead.]

152 **tretis** graceful

154 **sikerly** certainly

155 **a spanne** the width of a hand [The Prioress's wimple is very pleated.]

157 **fetis** neat, well-made

162 ***Amor vincit omnia*** Love conquers all

The Prioress is sentimental about animals. Her wimple is folded, maybe to show her forehead, and her figure is full – though it should really not have been visible. Her rosary (string of prayer beads) is more attractive than is perhaps warranted in an object to aid worship, and she has a golden brooch with an ambiguous message on it. She has a very large retinue accompanying her, perhaps more than was fitting her rank as the head of a convent.

But, for to speken of hire conscience,
She was so charitable and so pitous
She wolde wepe, if that she saugh a mous
Kaught in a trappe, if it were deed or bledde.   145
Of smale houndes hadde she that she fedde
With rosted flessh, or milk and wastel-breed.
But soore wepte she if oon of hem were deed,
Or if men smoot it with a yerde smerte;
And al was conscience and tendre herte.   150
Ful semely hir wimpul pinched was,
Hir nose tretis, hir eyen greye as glas,
Hir mouth ful smal, and therto softe and reed;
But sikerly she hadde a fair forheed;
It was almoost a spanne brood, I trowe;   155
For, hardily, she was nat undergrowe.
Ful fetis was hir cloke, as I was war.
Of smal coral aboute hire arm she bar
A peire of bedes, gauded al with grene,
And theron heng a brooch of gold ful sheene,   160
On which ther was first write a crowned A,
And after *Amor vincit omnia.*
Another Nonne with hire hadde she,
That was hir chapeleyne, and preestes thre.

Monks took vows of poverty, chastity, and obedience. Their business was to worship God through prayer, and in some orders through teaching and medicine. They usually took a vow of stability, promising to stay in the monastery for their whole lives. Monasteries provided shelter for travellers, and were the guardians of knowledge and education. Many people left land to monasteries, so that by Chaucer's time monks were landlords as well as farmers. Life for the monks became easier than the founders of the orders had foreseen.

- Read lines 169–72. Bells, graduated in matched sets and sounding in harmony, were an icon in mediaeval painting for the power of reason. What do you think would be the effect upon Chaucer's listeners of this complicated metaphor of church bells and harness bells?
- Read lines 173–82. This sounds like a contemptuous dismissal of his vocation by a cynical and corrupt monk. By Chaucer's day the monasteries had become rich and powerful through good management of their estates. In that case has the Monk got a point? Look at his argument as well as listening to his tone. (Whose voice do you think is putting the argument and setting the tone? Bear in mind that this was a poem to be recited.)
- Read lines 183–7. Who is talking here? What tone is indicated? What do you think is the significance for the Monk's argument of 'How shal the world be served?' (line 187)?

165	**a fair for the maistrie** outshining all others	174	**somedel streit** somewhat strict
166	**outridere** a monk who rode out to inspect the monastery's outlying estates	175	**leet olde thinges pace** let old things pass away
	venerie hunting, with a possible suggestion of 'venery' or sexual pleasure	176	**heeld after the newe world the space** followed the new way of thinking ['The space' means something like 'meanwhile'.]
168	**deyntee** excellent [He should not have owned one horse, let alone many.]	177	**yaf nat of that text a pulled hen** didn't give a plucked chicken for that rule
173	**Seint Maure** [one of Benedict's first followers, who brought the Rule to France]	179	**recchelees** not caring about rules
		180	**waterlees** out of water
	Seint Beneit Saint Benedict [He founded western monasticism in about AD 500, and wrote the Benedictine Rule by which monks lived. His rule was humane but demanding, and was often revived by monks who started new orders because they thought things had grown too lax in existing ones.]	182	**oystre** oyster [Oysters were plentiful and cheap.]
		184	**wood** mad
		186	**swinken** work
		187	**Austin** St Augustine [one of the great theologians of the early church]
			bit bade, instructed

The Monk is a strong middle-aged man who sees his vocation as a monk more as a career, and thinks he would make an ideal abbot – a very high rank, equal to a bishop.

A Monk ther was, a fair for the maistrie,   165
An outridere, that lovede venerie,
A manly man, to been an abbot able.
Ful many a deyntee hors hadde he in stable,
And whan he rood, men mighte his bridel heere
Ginglen in a whistlinge wind als cleere   170
And eek as loude as dooth the chapel belle
Ther as this lord was kepere of the celle.
The reule of Seint Maure or of Seint Beneit,
By cause that it was old and somdel streit
This ilke Monk leet olde thinges pace,   175
And heeld after the newe world the space.
He yaf nat of that text a pulled hen,
That seith that hunters ben nat hooly men,
Ne that a monk, whan he is recchelees,
Is likned til a fissh that is waterlees,—   180
This is to seyn, a monk out of his cloistre.
But thilke text heeld he nat worth an oystre;
And I seyde his opinion was good.
What sholde he studie and make himselven wood,
Upon a book in cloistre alwey to poure,   185
Or swinken with his handes, and laboure,
As Austin bit? How shal the world be served?

- What do you think is the tone of line 188? Who is talking now?
- What is suggested about the Monk in lines 193–9?
- What impression of the Monk's temperament and physical presence is given by lines 200–2?
- Compare the Monk's outlook and ability with the Knight's. How far, and in what ways, would it be suitable for them to change places?

188	**to him reserved** kept [for him to do himself]	
189	**prikasour** mounted huntsman	
191	**priking** spurring, hunting the hare	
192	**for no cost wolde he spare** would not give up hunting for anything	
193-4	**purfiled at the hond/With gris** trimmed at the wrist with expensive fur [against the Rule of Saint Benedict]	
196	**curious** elaborate and expensive	
197	**love-knotte** a love token, perhaps suggesting he is not chaste	
199	**as he hadde been enoint** shiny as if polished in oil [An ironical reference	

to the holy oil used to bestow blessing in religious ceremonies.]

200	**in good point** stout, with a rounded belly
201	**stepe** prominent, staring
202	**that stemed as a forneys of a leed** that shone like a furnace under a cauldron
204	**prelaat** a high-ranking churchman, such as an abbot
205	**forpined** thin from suffering
206	**a fat swan** [Swans were luxury food that normally only the nobility could afford.]
207	**palfrey** a high quality riding horse

'What sholde he studie and make himselven wood,
Upon a book in cloistre alwey to poure?'

The Monk's argument in favour of his way of life is completed, and there is a reminder of his
passion for hunting.

Lat Austin have his swink to him reserved!
Therfore he was a prikasour aright:
Grehoundes he hadde as swift as fowel in flight;   190
Of priking and of hunting for the hare
Was al his lust, for no cost wolde he spare.
I seigh his sleves purfiled at the hond
With gris, and that the fineste of a lond;
And, for to festne his hood under his chin,   195
He hadde of gold ywroght a ful curious pin;
A love-knotte in the gretter ende ther was.
His heed was balled, that shoon as any glas,
And eek his face, as he hadde been enoint.
He was a lord ful fat and in good point;   200
His eyen stepe, and rollinge in his heed,
That stemed as a forneys of a leed;
His bootes souple, his hors in greet estaat.
Now certeinly he was a fair prelaat;
He was nat pale as a forpined goost.   205
A fat swan loved he best of any roost.
His palfrey was as broun as is a berie.

31

- What impression of the Friar is given in lines 208–9? How far is it borne out in lines 210–39?
- Look at lines 225–32. From the tone of these lines, what do you think is Chaucer's view of the Friar?
- Make a list of the people the Friar dealt with, the ways in which he presented himself to them, and the ways in which he raised money from them.

208	**wantowne** someone disordered in behaviour
209	**ful solempne** deeply impressive
210	**ordres foure** [There were four separate orders of friars: Dominican, Franciscan, Carmelite and Austin (or Augustinian) Friars.]
211	**daliaunce and fair langage** gossip and fair speech [also suggests lovemaking and false promises]
212-13	**maad ful many a mariage ... owene cost** paid for girls to be settled in marriage [after he had seduced them]
214	**Unto his ordre he was a noble post** he was an honoured supporter or earner for his order
216	**frankeleyns** freeholders [men of some wealth]
219	**curat** ordinary parish priest
220	**licentiat** given a licence [to hear confessions]
222	**absolucioun** forgiveness for sins
224	**pitaunce** gift
226	**yshrive** absolved from sin
227	**make avaunt** be sure
228	**wiste** knew
232	**moote** may
	povre freres poor friars
233	**His tipet was ay farsed** his cape was always stuffed
236	**rote** small harp
237	**Of yeddinges he baar outrely the prys** he was the best ballad singer
239	**thereto** also

'Ful swetely herde he confessioun,
And plesaunt was his absolucioun'

The Friar is a member of a religious order dedicated to a life of poverty and service in the community, not in a monastery. He has been assigned an area by his order – his limits as a 'limitor' – where he operates. The Friar knows when to give a light penance to sinners, in return for suitably generous donations. His actions, especially to do with women and with landowners, are described as if eminently reasonable.

A Frere ther was, a wantowne and a merie,
A limitour, a ful solempne man.
In alle the ordres foure is noon that kan   210
So muchel of daliaunce and fair langage.
He hadde maad ful many a mariage
Of yonge wommen at his owene cost.
Unto his ordre he was a noble post.
Ful wel biloved and famulier was he   215
With frankeleyns over al in his contree,
And eek with worthy wommen of the toun;
For he hadde power of confessioun,
As seyde himself, moore than a curat,
For of his ordre he was licenciat.   220
Ful swetely herde he confessioun,
And plesaunt was his absolucioun:
He was an esy man to yeve penaunce,
Ther as he wiste to have a good pitaunce.
For unto a povre ordre for to yive   225
Is signe that a man is wel yshrive;
For if he yaf, he dorste make avaunt,
He wiste that a man was repentaunt;
For many a man so hard is of his herte,
He may nat wepe, althogh him soore smerte.   230
Therfore in stede of wepinge and preyeres
Men moote yeve silver to the povre freres.
His tipet was ay farsed ful of knives
And pinnes, for to yeven faire wives.
And certeinly he hadde a murie note: 235
Wel koude he singe and pleyen on a rote;
Of yeddinges he baar outrely the prys.
His nekke whit was as the flour-de-lys;
Therto he strong was as a champioun.

- Read lines 240–8. Whose voice are we hearing? What impression of the Friar do you receive from these lines?
- The Friar is very successful, in his own terms. What aspects of the Friar's position, behaviour and appearance would have hidden his vices and made him attractive to the people he was exploiting? List his vices and his attractive qualities.
- What do you think are the similarities and differences between the Friar and the Squire?
- Discuss the implications of the simile in lines 269–70.
- Do you think Chaucer approved of friars in general? List the evidence, for and against.
- Make a list of the reasons why you think the Friar is on the pilgrimage.
- Discuss with a partner the qualities you might expect a religious person to have. Then taking the three characters in turn, the Prioress, the Monk and the Friar, list the qualities Chaucer attributes to him or her, paying particular attention to the first thing he says about each.

241–2 **(knew) everich hostiler... or a beggestere** (knew) every landlord and barmaid better than he did lepers or female beggars

244 **facultee** profession

247 **poraille** the poor

248 **vitaille** provisions

251 **vertuous** both 'gentlemanly' and 'virtuous'

253 **yaf a certeyn ferme** paid rent

256 *In principio* In the beginning [opening of St John's Gospel]

257 **ferthing** a small coin

258 **His purchas was well bettre than his rente** his income was greater than his rent [He made more than he gave to his order for the right to his limit or district.]

259 **And rage he koude, as it were right a whelp** he could play like a puppy

260 **love-dayes** special days for settling quarrels

262 **cope** cape

263 **maister** Master of Arts

264 **semicope** short cape

266 **lipsed, for his wantownesse** lisped affectedly

The Friar's contradictory qualities are further developed in the description of his activities and his manner. His contempt for the poor and sick, and his fawning on the wealthy, are made very clear. He knows how to please all sorts of people but he has no respect for them, and no conscience about taking what little they have.

He knew the tavernes wel in every toun   240
And everich hostiler and tappestere
Bet than a lazar or a beggestere;
For unto swich a worthy man as he
Acorded nat, as by his facultee,
To have with sike lazars aqueyntaunce.   245
It is nat honest, it may nat avaunce,
For to deelen with no swich poraille,
But al with riche and selleres of vitaille.
And over al, ther as profit sholde arise,
Curteis he was and lowely of servise.   250
Ther nas no man nowher so vertuous.
He was the beste beggere in his hous;
And yaf a certeyn ferme for the graunt;
Noon of his bretheren cam ther in his haunt;
For thogh a widwe hadde noght a sho,   255
So plesaunt was his '*In principio*,'
Yet wolde he have a ferthing, er he wente.
His purchas was wel bettre than his rente.
And rage he koude, as it were right a whelp.
In love-dayes ther koude he muchel help,   260
For ther he was nat lik a cloisterer
With a thredbare cope, as is a povre scoler,
But he was lyk a maister or a pope.
Of double worstede was his semicope,
That rounded as a belle out of the presse.   265
Somwhat he lipsed, for his wantownesse,
To make his Englissh sweete upon his tonge;
And in his harping, whan that he hadde songe,
His eyen twinkled in his heed aright,
As doon the sterres in the frosty night.   270
This worthy limitour was cleped Huberd.

- We learn a number of things about the Merchant's appearance and manner of speech. How would you summarise the image he projects?
- What seems to be his business? List the evidence.
- Read lines 281–4 aloud, looking carefully at the punctuation, and listening to the flow of the language. What impression of the Merchant's character does Chaucer give in these lines? Write a paragraph explaining how Chaucer achieves this.
- The Merchant is a successful man in a commercially confident and progressive age. Read the section on page 93 and then write a brief account of how the Merchant's way of life might or might not fit into the social structure of the time.
- What is the effect, in your view, of the use of 'solompnely' and the repeated use of 'worthy' in this portrait? Do these words have a shade of meaning arising from their earlier use in connection with the Friar and with other characters, or with the Merchant's success in his profession?
- What values do you think might have prompted the Merchant to join the pilgrimage?

273	**mottelee** motley [cloth woven from threads of two colours]	
274	**Flaundrissh bever hat** expensive hat made from beaver skin from Flanders	
277	**Sowninge alwey th'encrees of his winning** always proclaiming the growth of his profits	
280	**Wel koude he in eschaunge sheeldes selle** he was skilled in dealing in	foreign currency ['Sheeldes' were units of exchange named after French or Flemish coins. This kind of currency dealing could verge on the illegal, and was often regarded as unethical.]
		281	**bisette** used
		284	**chevissaunce** dealings in money
		286	**noot** know not

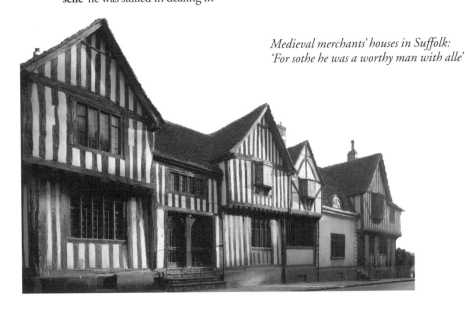

Medieval merchants' houses in Suffolk:
'For sothe he was a worthy man with alle'

Chaucer does not perhaps intend us to take the Merchant at his own valuation, but his
treatment of this character is – like the man – not straightforward. The character is secretive
and dignified: his social status, bolstered by his apparent wealth, is high. The Merchant talks
weightily, mostly about his growing profits, and is anxious for the sea lanes to be kept open
between Orewelle (near Ipswich) and Middelburgh (in Holland), to serve his trade. Behind
his impressive exterior, however, lies the fact that he is in debt.

A Marchant was ther with a forked berd,
In mottelee, and hye on horse he sat;
Upon his heed a Flaundrissh bever hat,
His bootes clasped faire and fetisly. 275
His resons he spak ful solempnely,
Sowninge alwey th'encrees of his winning.
He wolde the see were kept for any thing
Bitwixe Middelburgh and Orewelle.
Wel koude he in eschaunge sheeldes selle. 280
This worthy man ful wel his wit bisette:
Ther wiste no wight that he was in dette,
So estatly was he of his governaunce
With his bargaines and with his chevissaunce.
For sothe he was a worthy man with alle, 285
But, sooth to seyn, I noot how men him calle.

- What do you think are the Clerk's motives for joining the pilgrimage?
- Is there anything for which you would criticise the Clerk?
- Clerks would earlier almost automatically become priests. Is there, in your view, anything in Chaucer's description that might be seen as criticism of the Clerk for not doing so?
- The word 'philosopher' in Chaucer's day meant something like the modern sense of the word, but included someone who sought to turn base metal into gold by various chemical and magical means and then sold the 'secret' to gullible people. What do you think is the effect of the allusion to philosophers in this description?

288 **That unto logik hadde longe ygo** had long since reached the study of logic [Medieval education had two courses: the Trivium consisting of grammar, logic and rhetoric – later dismissed as elementary, or 'trivial'; and the Quadrivium consisting of arithmetic, geometry, astronomy and music.]

290 **nas** was not ('ne was')

291 **holwe, and therto sobrely** thin, and moreover serious

292 **overeste courtepy** outermost garment

293 **geten him yet no benefice** had so far no living or appointment as a curate

294 **have office** have a non-religious appointment [such as working in the royal administration]

295 **him was levere** he would rather

296 **Twenty bookes, clad in blak or reed** twenty books bound in black or red [an enormous number, considering the cost of books, each copy of which had to be written out by hand]

297 **Aristotle** [Greek philosopher (384–22 BC) whose books influenced much medieval thought]

298 **fithele** violin (fiddle)

sautrie psaltery, a stringed instument

299 **But al be that** although he was ['Although' here is ironic: the sense is 'because he was a philosopher, he had little gold'.]

300 **cofre** money box

301 **hente** get or take [Scholars had to depend on friends and relatives for money, repaying gifts with prayers.]

304 **scoleye** study [In Chaucer's times education was available only through the church, and if anyone wanted to study, as this Clerk does, he had to take holy orders.]

305 **cure** care

307 **forme and reverence** due form and respect

308-9 **short and quik and ful ... vertu was his speche** his speech was brief and economical, full of thoughtful observations and judgements

The Clerk is a scholar, devoted to the study of logic, and although he prays for his benefactors, he is drawn to learning and teaching, rather than to active priesthood. A large part of the description of him is occupied by what he does not have – although he does have a passion for books. He is an extreme example of an unworldly scholar: very poor and totally uninterested in advancing his career. Intense and sparing with words, the Clerk is described as an ideal, and as a man almost comically uninterested in worldly matters. Not only is he dressed in worn clothing, but he and his horse are thin to the point of emaciation. There could not be a more complete contrast to the Merchant.

A Clerk ther was of Oxenford also,
That unto logik hadde longe ygo.
As leene was his hors as is a rake,   ·
And he nas nat right fat, I undertake,   290
But looked holwe, and therto sobrely.
Ful thredbare was his overeste courtepy;
For he hadde geten him yet no benefice,
Ne was so worldly for to have office.
For him was levere have at his beddes heed   295
Twenty bookes, clad in blak or reed,
Of Aristotle and his philosophie,
Than robes riche, or fithele, or gay sautrie.
But al be that he was a philosophre,
Yet hadde he but litel gold in cofre;   300
But al that he mighte of his freendes hente,
On bookes and on lerninge he it spente,
And bisily gan for the soules preye
Of hem that yaf him wherwith to scoleye.
Of studie took he moost cure and moost heede.   305
Noght o word spak he moore than was neede,
And that was seyd in forme and reverence,
And short and quik and ful of hy sentence;
Sowninge in moral vertu was his speche,
And gladly wolde he lerne and gladly teche.   310

- The tone does not seem ironic at the start. What is the effect of 'semed' on line 315 and again on line 324?
- Sergeants at law had to spend many years studying before attaining this rank, from which judges were selected. They were therefore likely to come from a moneyed background. Where does Chaucer suggest the Sergeant's abilities lay?
- How much of this description do you think would be pleasing to the Sergeant?
- What values, in your view, might have drawn the Sergeant to the pilgrimage?

312 **at the Parvis** in the porch of St Paul's Cathedral [a regular place for lawyers to meet clients]

313 **riche of excellence** of great talent [with a pun on 'riche']

316 **justice** judge

assise Assize Courts [for hearing civil cases]

317 **By patente and by pleyn commissioun** by open (patent) letter of appointment from the King, and by personal commission from the King to hear all cases

318 **science** expert knowledge

renoun reputation

319 **Of fees and robes had he many oon** he had many annual retainers of clothing and money from several great men for his legal services throughout the year

320 **so greet a purchasour** so great a buyer of land [on behalf of his client, or for himself]

321 **Al was fee simple to him** absolute possession [of the land – with a pun on 'easy money']

322 **His purchasing mighte nat been infect** there was no disputing ownership of land deals he had arranged

325-6 **In termes hadde ... king William were falle** He knew all the detail of the cases and judgments made since the time of William [the Conqueror]

327 **Therto he koude endite** he also knew how to draw up legal documents

328 **no wighte pinche at his writing** no-one could challenge the correctness of his legal documents

329 **koude he pleyn by rote** could he recite (accurately) by heart

330-1 **He rood ... barres smale** he rode informally wearing a coat of mixed colours, belted with a silk sash with narrow stripes

The Sergeant at Law as depicted in the Ellesmere manuscript: 'He rood but hoomly in a medlee cote'

The Sergeant of the Law ranks very highly, being on an equal footing with the Knight; unlike the Knight, he is not an ideal. The abilities of the Sergeant of the Law are described very briefly and incompletely, and we learn nothing of his appearance, but Chaucer suggests his withdrawn and cautious nature ('war and wys'), and hints at his readiness to make money from every transaction.

A Sergeant of the Lawe, war and wys,
That often hadde been at the Parvis,
Ther was also, ful riche of excellence.
Discreet he was and of greet reverence—
He semed swich, his wordes weren so wise.   315
Justice he was ful often in assise,
By patente and by pleyn commissioun.
For his science and for his heigh renoun,
Of fees and robes hadde he many oon.
So greet a purchasour was nowher noon: 320
Al was fee simple to him in effect;
His purchasing mighte nat been infect.
Nowher so bisy a man as he ther nas,
And yet he semed bisier than he was.
In termes hadde he caas and doomes alle   325
That from the time of king William were falle.
Therto he koude endite, and make a thing,
Ther koude no wight pinche at his writing;
And every statut koude he pleyn by rote
He rood but hoomly in a medlee cote,   330
Girt with a ceint of silk, with barres smale;
Of his array telle I no lenger tale.

- What impression do you receive of the Franklin as a person? Look back to the descriptions of the Friar and the Monk. In comparison to these, what sort of detail does Chaucer not reveal about the Franklin?
- What does the extraordinary abundance of food in the Franklin's house tell us about him? What motive, other than his Epicurean principles, could he have had for keeping such a full and expensive table?
- Look back at Chaucer's views on the Knight and the Friar, and the way in which he expresses them; then list what you think might be the Franklin's good and bad points.

336   **by the morwe** first thing in the morning

      a sop in wyn bread dipped in wine

337   **evere his wone** always his habit or custom

338   **Epicurus owene sone** a true son of Epicurus [Greek philosopher who was associated with the enjoyment of bodily pleasures]

339–40   **that pleyn delit/Was verray felicitee parfit** that full gratification of the senses was the highest form of happiness [*literally*: that full delight was true perfect felicity. The true nature of felicity is a major theme throughout *The Canterbury Tales*.]

342   **Seint Julian** [the patron saint of hospitality]

      contree country [in sense of region, or home ground]

343   **after oon** consistently good

344   **envined** stocked with wine

346   **flessh** meat

348   **deyntees** choice food

349   **after the sondry sesons** according to the various seasons

350   **so chaunged he his mete and soper** he changed his dishes and menus [*literally*: his food and suppers]

351   **muwe** mews or cage

352   **luce in stewe** pike in fishpond [Fishponds and dovecotes were a source of fresh food, particularly during the lean times of the year when salted meat was unobtainable.]

353   **Wo was his cook** his cook was in trouble

354   **poynaunt** sharp, well seasoned

355   **table dormant** fixed table [always ready, as opposed to the more usual demountable tables of the time]

357   **sessiouns** sessions of the magistrate's court

358   **knight of the shire** Member of Parliament for his county [Chaucer shares a number of attributes with the Franklin.]

359   **anlaas** dagger

      gipser purse

361   **shirreve** sheriff, responsible to the Crown for law and order in his county [The Franklin has money and land, he holds important positions, but he is not gentry. He might perhaps be seen as an indication of a new social order in which money and land are increasingly important.]

      contour auditor, accountant

The Franklin, a landowning country squire ranking below the gentry, is an uncomplicated character. According to the beliefs of the time, his temperament is made from a balance of four elements: air, fire, earth and water. These were associated with the four 'humours' – blood, phlegm, choler (anger) and bile. The Franklin has a happy or 'sangwyn' character because blood (Latin 'sanguis') predominates. His red face, set off by the whiteness of his hair, shows his hot and moist 'complexioun'. The Franklin is a generous host, and a lover of good cooking. He is also a conscientious servant of the law and of the King.

A Frankeleyn was in his compaignie.
Whit was his berd as is the dayesie;
Of his complexioun he was sangwin.   335
Wel loved he by the morwe a sop in wyn;
To liven in delit was evere his wone,
For he was Epicurus owene sone,
That heeld opinioun that pleyn delit
Was verray felicitee parfit.   340
An housholdere, and that a greet, was he;
Seint Julian he was in his contree.
His breed, his ale, was alweys after oon;
A bettre envined man was nowher noon.
Withoute bake mete was nevere his hous   345
Of fissh and flessh, and that so plentevous,
It snewed in his hous of mete and drinke,
Of alle deyntees that men koude thinke.
After the sondry sesons of the yeer,
So chaunged he his mete and his soper.   350
Ful many a fat partrich hadde he in muwe,
And many a breem and many a luce in stuwe.
Wo was his cook but if his sauce were
Poynaunt and sharp, and redy al his geere.
His table dormant in his halle alway   355
Stood redy covered al the longe day.
At sessiouns ther was he lord and sire;
Ful ofte time he was knight of the shire.
An anlaas and a gipser al of silk
Heeng at his girdel, whit as morne milk.   360
A shirreve hadde he been, and a contour.
Was nowher swich a worthy vavasour.

- What is the effect of the detailed description of the Guildsmen's clothing and equipment?
- What evidence can you find of the social status of the Guildsmen and their wives, or of the social status they would like to have?
- What impression of the Cook – apart from his obvious grossness – do you receive from this short description?

366   **solempne** dignified [Chaucer's ironic use of this word becomes clearer as his description continues.]

367   **apiked** ornamented

368–9   **Hir knives were ... al with silver** their knives were not inlaid with brass but with silver [They were technically breaking the law in carrying decorated knives – such ornamentation was reserved for the gentry and above.]

370   **everydeel** completely, in every way

371–2   **well semed ech ... on a deis** each of them seemed to be a citizen fit to sit on a platform in a town hall [*literally*: a fine burgess to sit on a dais in a guildhall, i.e. fit to run the affairs of their trade association]

373–4   **Everich, for the ... been an alderman** each of them, on account of his experience and knowledge, was suitable to be an alderman [No such tradesmen were elected to be aldermen (senior councillors) in London until long after Chaucer's time.]

375   **for catel hadde they ynogh and rente** they had enough goods and income from rents to qualify as aldermen

376–7   **and eek hir ... they to blame** and also their wives would certainly approve [if they were to become aldermen]; if they did not they [the husbands] would certainly be blamed [by their wives]

378   **ycleped 'madame'** called 'madame' [An alderman was the lowest rank to be accorded the courtesy of having his wife addressed in this way.]

379   **and goon to vigilies al bifore** be placed first in the procession to mass on vigils of important saints' days. [Vigils were the day before the actual feast.]

380   **have a mantel roialliche ybore** to have one's cloak ceremonially carried like royalty [*literally*: royally carried]

382   **marybones** marrow bones

383   **poudre-marchant tart** a sharp [tart] spice

     galingale Indian root used to flavour food

384   **wel koude he knowe** he was an experienced judge [with the suggestion that he was a drunkard]

385   **sethe** boil

386   **mortreux** stew or thick soup

     pie a meat pie [Fruit pies were introduced later.]

388   **mormal** a sore full of pus

389   **blancmanger** a thick stew of meat or fish, highly flavoured with spice

The Haberdasher, the Carpenter, the Webbe (weaver), the Dyer and the Tapicer (tapestry maker) are members of a religious guild, i.e. a guild belonging to a particular parish rather than a specific trade. Such guilds also acted as friendly societies, helping their members and their members' families in hard times. The five Guildsmen are introduced as a whole, with only their different jobs to distinguish them. Chaucer describes them showing off, even though there is no-one around to recognise them. They have their own cook with them, about whom Chaucer has reservations, even though he is good at his job.

   An Haberdasshere and a Carpenter,
A Webbe, a Dyere, and a Tapicer,—
And they were clothed alle in o liveree   365
Of a solempne and a greet fraternitee.
Ful fressh and newe hir geere apiked was;
Hir knives were chaped noght with bras
But al with silver; wroght ful clene and weel
Hire girdles and hir pouches everydeel.   370
Wel semed ech of hem a fair burgeys
To sitten in a yeldehalle on a deis.
Everich, for the wisdom that he kan,
Was shaply for to been an alderman.
For catel hadde they ynogh and rente,   375
And eek hir wives wolde it wel assente;
And elles certeyn were they to blame.
It is ful fair to been ycleped 'madame,'
And goon to vigilies al bifore,
And have a mantel roialliche ybore.   380
A Cook they hadde with hem for the nones
To boille the chiknes with the marybones,
And poudre-marchant tart and galingale.
Wel koude he knowe a draughte of Londoun ale.
He koude rooste, and sethe, and broille, and frie,   385
Maken mortreux, and wel bake a pie.
But greet harm was it, as it thoughte me,
That on his shine a mormal hadde he.
For blankmanger, that made he with the beste.

Coats of arms of medieval guilds

- Read lines 390–1. What does this suggest to you about Chaucer's view of the Shipman or of people from Dartmouth?
- List your impressions of the Shipman, first from lines 390–3, then from 394–5, then 396–9, and finally from 400–2.
- How would you describe the effect of Chaucer's brief statement in line 402?

390 **woninge fer by weste** living in the far west of England

392 **He rood upon a rouncy, as he kouthe** he rode on a carthorse, as best he could

393 **falding** a tough woollen cloth

394 **laas** a lace or lanyard

395 **under his arm adoun** under his arm [concealed but ready for instant use]

396 **maad his hewe al broun** made his colour brown, sunburned

397 **felawe** friend or acquaintance, with overtones of low class or disreputable

399 **fro Burdeux-ward, whil that the chapman sleep** on the journey from Bordeaux, while the merchant slept [There was much trade in wine with France, and the Shipman obviously took the chance to drink his share.]

400 **of nice conscience took he no keep** he paid no attention to tender conscience ['nice' means scrupulous]

401 **hyer hond** if he won [*literally:* the upper hand]

402 **By water he sente hem hoom to every lond** he threw them overboard and drowned them [*literally:* he sent them home by water to every country]

403 **rekene** calculate, predict

404 **stremes** rivers

daungers hazards

405 **his herbewe, and his moone, his lodemenage** his knowledge of harbours, of the moon (and its influence on tides) and of navigation [This is the Shipman's professional knowledge, emphasised by Chaucer's use of 'his'.]

406 **Ther nas noon swich** there was no-one to match him

Cartage Cartagena in Spain

407 **wys to undertake** reliable in dealing with a task

408 **berd** beard

409 **havenes** harbours

410 **Gootlond** Gotland, [a Swedish island, or possibly Jutland in Denmark]

Finistere a headland in Spain

411 **crike** creek or inlet

Britaigne Brittany, in France

412 **barge** ship

ycleped called, named

Maudelaine St Mary Magdalene [pronounced then as Chaucer spells it]

An astrolabe, an early instrument of navigation: 'But of his craft to rekene wel his tides, ... His herbewe, and his moone, his lodemenage'

The Shipman has a vast experience of coasts, harbours, tides and navigation, but is not at home on land; certainly not on a horse. His knowledge encompasses the North Sea, the coasts of France and Spain and even some parts of the Mediterranean. He would have had to carry all this knowledge in his mind, with few instruments or charts to help him. Chaucer tells us, almost casually, of his activities when clear of land.

A Shipman was ther, woninge fer by weste;   390
For aught I woot, he was of Dertemouthe.
He rood upon a rouncy, as he kouthe,
In a gowne of falding to the knee.
A daggere hanginge on a laas hadde he
Aboute his nekke, under his arm adoun.   395
The hoote somer hadde maad his hewe al broun;
And certeinly he was a good felawe.
Ful many a draughte of wyn had he ydrawe
Fro Burdeux-ward, whil that the chapman sleep.
Of nice conscience took he no keep.   400
If that he faught, and hadde the hyer hond,
By water he sente hem hoom to every lond.
But of his craft to rekene wel his tides,
His stremes, and his daungers him bisides,
His herberwe, and his moone, his lodemenage,   405
Ther nas noon swich from Hulle to Cartage.
Hardy he was and wys to undertake;
With many a tempest hadde his berd been shake.
He knew alle the havenes, as they were,
Fro Gootlond to the cape of Finistere,   410
And every crike in Britaigne and in Spaine.
His barge ycleped was the Maudelaine.

Medicine in Chaucer's day was regulated by knowledge derived from authoritative books written in classical times (many of which are listed by Chaucer), along with a few written more recently. The references to astrology were standard in the medicine of the time, and much diagnosis and treatment depended on the outcome of this kind of 'magik natureel', i.e. good magic as opposed to black magic. The references to the humours (see page 43) indicate the extent of the Doctor's knowledge: there is no branch of his profession in which he is not an expert.

• Read lines 414–15 again. The verb 'to speke' might mean 'when we are talking about' or it could mean 'for talking about'. In the light of the rest of the description of the Doctor, consider the evidence for both these readings. You might consider, for example, what Chaucer means when he calls the Doctor a 'verray, parfit praktisour'.

415	**phisik** medicine
417–18	**He kepte ... magik natureel** he looked after his patients with great care, working by the astrological hours, using his natural magic
419	**Wel koude ... ascendent** he could skilfully calculate the (astrological) ascendant
421	**everich maladie** every illness
422	**Were it of hoot, or coold** [An individual's humours, and therefore the balance of his or her health, could be affected by the position of the planets (e.g. Mars is hot and dry), by the signs of the zodiac (e.g. Aries is also hot and dry), by the season of the year (e.g. summer is hot and dry), by the time of day (see the reference to 'hours' in line 418) and by diet. If illness was the result of the humours being out of balance,

it was the Doctor's task to find out why and provide remedial treatment to restore the balance.]

423	**engendred** were produced
425	**the cause yknowe, and of his harm the roote** once he knew the source of the illness and the origin of its harm
426	**Anon he yaf the sike man his boote** he immediately gave the sick man his remedy [perhaps a cure, or perhaps a medicine from the apothecary, with whom he is in financial partnership]
427	**apothecaries** druggists, pharmacists
428	**letuaries** remedies
429	**winne** profit
430	**Hir frendshipe nas not newe to beginne** their friendship (partnership) was no recent thing

The Doctor's great expertise is praised and celebrated; it apparently extends to a clear grasp of how to profit from his work.

With us ther was a Doctour of Phisik;
In al this world ne was ther noon him lik,
To speke of phisik and of surgerye,   415
For he was grounded in astronomye.
He kepte his pacient a ful greet deel
In houres by his magik natureel.
Wel koude he fortunen the ascendent
Of his images for his pacient.   420
He knew the cause of everich maladie,
Were it of hoot, or coold, or moist, or drie,
And where they engendred, and of what humour.
He was a verray, parfit praktisour:
The cause yknowe, and of his harm the roote,   425
Anon he yaf the sike man his boote.
Ful redy hadde he his apothecaries
To sende him drogges and his letuaries,
For ech of hem made oother for to winne—
Hir frendshipe nas nat newe to biginne.   430

'He knew the cause of everich maladie'

- Whose voice do you think we are hearing when the list of authorities is being recited (lines 431–6)?
- What do you think the Doctor wanted people to think of him? Write a brief response, referring in detail to the text for evidence of your view.
- Do you think there is anything in Chaucer's description of the Doctor that he would object to?
- In what ways do you think the Doctor might be compared to the Shipman, another master of his craft?
- What values do you think prompted the Doctor to go on the pilgrimage?

431–6 [Some of these authorities date from classical times: **Esculapius** was the Greek god of medicine; **Ypocras** was Hippocrates, originator of the Hippocratic oath taken by doctors; **Galen** was a Roman doctor of the first century AD whose works were fundamental to medicine for many centuries. Other names are later Arabian and Persian writers, and the last three lived shortly before Chaucer's time – **Bernard** was Scottish and **Gatesden** and **Gilbertin** were English.]

437 **mesurable** temperate, careful

438–9 **For it was of ... and digestible** he did not eat very much but his food was very nutritious and easily digestible

441 **sangwin** scarlet cloth

pers blue-grey cloth

442 **taffata and sendal** silks [For someone reluctant to spend, the doctor spent lavishly on his clothes.]

444 **He kepte that he wan in pestilence** he kept all he earned during times of plague [rather than giving to relieve distress. This would have had a very strong resonance in Chaucer's time, when the Black Death was a horror still in living memory.]

445 **gold in phisik is a cordial** [Gold given in a drink was thought of as a remedy of great effectiveness. Its great price would also have interested the Doctor. Compare this with the description of the Clerk, lines 299–300.]

446 **in special** particularly

The pre-Christian origin of much of their knowledge gave doctors a reputation for atheism, which might account for the fact that 'his studie was but litel on the Bible' (line 440). The list of his authorities is impressive, and he evidently takes good care of his own health. The description ends with a cold emphasis on his love of money and good clothes.

Wel knew he the olde Esculapius,
And Deiscorides, and eek Rufus,
Olde Ypocras, Hali, and Galien,
Serapion, Razis, and Avicen,
Averrois, Damascien, and Constantin,   435
Bernard, and Gatesden, and Gilbertin.
Of his diete mesurable was he,
For it was of no superfluitee,
But of greet norissing and digestible.
His studie was but litel on the Bible.   440
In sangwin and in pers he clad was al,
Lined with taffata and with sendal;
And yet he was but esy of dispence;
He kepte that he wan in pestilence.
For gold in phisik is a cordial,   445
Therefore he lovede gold in special.

- List all the details Chaucer tells us about the Wife, and write a detailed prose version of her appearance and character.

447 **good Wif** mistress of a house [a substantial status]
biside near

448 **somdel deef** partially deaf
scathe a pity

449 **haunt** skill [Are we perhaps hearing her own view of herself here?]

452 **That to the offringe bifore hire sholde goon** [People approached the altar with their offering at Mass according to rank.]

453 **wrooth** furious

454 **out of alle charitee** angry and full of hard thoughts [not in a proper spiritual state to make an offering]

455 **coverchiefs** cloths arranged on wire frames [to make much satirised head-dresses]
ground texture

458 **fyn scarlet reed** [The colour of her stockings suggest her self-confidence and hint at her moral character.]

459 **streite yteyd** tightly fastened, possibly tightly stretched [the Wife is not a small woman]

459 **moiste** supple [expensive shoes, made of supple new leather]

461 **worthy** [a word to ponder each time Chaucer uses it]

462 **housbondes at chirche dore** [The marriage service for commoners took place at the church door.]

463–4 **nedeth nat to speke as nowthe** there's no need to go into that [a hint of a more irregular life]

465 **thries** thrice, three times

466 **passed many a straunge strem** crossed many a foreign river, travelled widely

467 **Boloigne** Boulogne in France

468 **Galice at Seinte-Jame, and at Coloigne** the shrine of the apostle James at Compostela in Galicia, north-west Spain, and at Cologne in Germany

469 **she koude muchel** she knew a great deal [ambiguous, suggesting moral and geographical wandering]

470 **gat-tothed** [Gaps between the teeth were thought to suggest a wanton or immoral character.]

471 **amblere** an easy-paced horse that moves both legs on one side simultaneously [comfortable to ride]

472 **ywimpled** a wimple, a garment resembling a nun's head-dress
heed head

473 **brood as is a bokeler or a targe** as wide as a shield or a target [a suggestion of a warlike character]

474 **foot-mantel** an outer coat

475 **spores** spurs [unnecessary on an ambler]

476 **felaweshipe** company
carpe talk, gossip

477–8 **Of remedies ... the olde daunce** it is possible she knew the remedies of love [aphrodisiacs and seduction techniques] for she knew all the arts of that activity

The Wife of Bath is another character who surpasses everyone in what she does – in this case the weaving of cloth, in which she has the reputation of outclassing the acknowledged experts of Ypres and Ghent. Her extraordinary, outsize and wilful character is sketched, and her rather worldly knowledge of the dance of love contrasts strongly with the Squire's heroic and courtly preoccupation with love.

A good Wif was ther of biside Bathe,
But she was somdel deef, and that was scathe.
Of clooth-making she hadde swich an haunt,
She passed hem of Ypres and of Gaunt.   450
In al the parisshe wif ne was ther noon
That to the offringe bifore hire sholde goon;
And if ther dide, certeyn so wrooth was she,
That she was out of alle charitee.
Hir coverchiefs ful fine weren of ground;   455
I dorste swere they weyeden ten pound
That on a Sonday weren upon hir heed.
Hir hosen weren of fyn scarlet reed,
Ful streite yteyd, and shoes ful moiste and newe.
Boold was hir face, and fair, and reed of hewe.   460
She was a worthy womman al hir live:
Housbondes at chirche dore she hadde five,
Withouten oother compaignye in youthe,—
But therof nedeth nat to speke as nowthe.
And thries hadde she been at Jerusalem;   465
She hadde passed many a straunge strem;
At Rome she hadde been, and at Boloigne,
In Galice at Seint-Jame, and at Coloigne.
She koude muchel of wandringe by the weye.
Gat-tothed was she, soothly for to seye.   470
Upon an amblere esily she sat,
Ywimpled wel, and on hir heed an hat
As brood as is a bokeler or a targe;
A foot-mantel aboute hir hipes large,
And on hir feet a paire of spores sharpe.   475
In felaweshipe wel koude she laughe and carpe.
Of remedies of love she knew per chaunce,
For she koude of that art the olde daunce.

- The description is wholly of the Parson's spiritual and moral qualities, yet this is one of the most clearly-drawn individual characters in The General Prologue. How would you describe the Parson's character in your own words?
- Apart from the obvious motive of prayer and thanksgiving, what do you think could be the Parson's reason for being on the pilgrimage?

480   **povre persoun of a toun** a poor priest (parson) in a parish

482   **clerk** an educated man

484   **parisshens** parishioners

485   **benigne** kindly, of good will
      wonder marvellously, wonderfully

487   **ypreved ofte sithes** proved many times over

488   **Ful looth were him to cursen for his tithes** very reluctant to excommunicate those who were late with their tithes [Priests' incomes derived from a payment of one tenth or tithe of their parishioners' produce, which many would or could not always pay. The priest was supposed to withdraw the comforts of religion, especially the sacraments, from late payers. It was a system open to abuse.]

489–91 **But rather wolde ... eek of his substaunce** he would certainly rather give, from the Easter money he received for his own keep, and even from his own possessions, to the poor parishioners around him

492   **he koude in litel thing have suffisaunce** very little was enough to satisfy him

493   **wyd** large
      fer asonder far-flung, widely spread

494   **ne lefte nat, for reyn ne thonder** did not neglect, not even in rain or thunder

495   **meschief** misfortune

496   **ferreste** furthest, most distant
      muche and lite rich and poor [*literally*: great and small]

497   **upon his feet** on foot [he had no horse]
      staf staff [a reminder of the shepherd's crook, symbol of Christ the Good Shepherd]

498   **ensample** example
      to his sheep he yaf he gave to his parishioners ['Sheep' is the term used by Christ for the souls in a priest's care, his 'flock'. The language used by, or about, the Parson, is Biblical and religious, emphasising his priorities, just as talk of money emphasises the main interest of many of the other pilgrims.]

499   **That first ... he taughte** first he did the right thing, then he taught people

501   **figure** saying, figure of speech

502   **iren** iron [If priests are weak in the face of temptation, how can ordinary people be expected to remain pure?]

The portrait of the Parson is wholly good, without a hint of irony. Around him faith and pastoral care seem to be failing, but he does not falter. Many of his good qualities are described in reverse, as failings he did not possess, which suggests that other priests did possess them, and were not so steadfast in their faith or practice. He remains in his humble parish, and is shown as a shepherd with his staff, imitating Christ in his care for his flock.

A good man was ther of religioun,
And was a povre Persoun of a toun,   480
But riche he was of hooly thoght and werk,
He was also a lerned man, a clerk,
That Cristes gospel trewely wolde preche;
His parisshens devoutly wolde he teche.
Benigne he was, and wonder diligent,   485
And in adversitee ful pacient,
And swich he was ypreved ofte sithes.
Ful looth were him to cursen for his tithes,
But rather wolde he yeven, out of doute,
Unto his povre parisshens aboute   490
Of his offring and eek of his substaunce.
He koude in litel thing have suffisaunce.
Wyd was his parisshe, and houses fer asonder,
But he ne lefte nat, for reyn ne thonder,
In siknesse nor in meschief to visite   495
The ferreste in his parisshe, muche and lite,
Upon his feet, and in his hand a staf.
This noble ensample to his sheep he yaf,
That first he wroghte, and afterward he taughte.
Out of the gospel he tho wordes caughte,   500
And this figure he added eek therto,
That if gold ruste, what shal iren do?

- Is there anything, in your view, about Chaucer's description of the Parson to suggest what he thought or felt about the abuses of the priesthood that he mentions?
- Write your own account of a corrupt priest, using the information provided by Chaucer in his description of the Parson.

504 **lewed** ignorant

505 **take keep** take note

506 **shiten** defiled, filthy

509 **He sette nat his benefice to hire** he did not install a curate, paying him part of his stipend [So that he could leave the work while still retaining the privileges of being parish priest. This sort of absenteeism was common in Chaucer's time and much criticised.]

510 **leet** left

511 **Seinte Poules** Saint Paul's

512 **chaunterie for soules** a chantry or chapel [where he could be paid for praying for some rich person's soul]

513 **with a bretherhed to been witholde** to be employed as a private priest to some brotherhood or guild

514 **folde** sheep fold

515 **miscarie** do it harm

518 **despitous** harsh, severe

519 **Ne of his speche daungerous ne digne** neither disdainful nor proud in talking to them

520 **discreet and benigne** courteous and kindly

523 **but it were** unless it were

524 **what so he were** no matter what sort of person he was

525 **snibben** rebuke

for the nonis immediately

526 **trowe** believe

527 **He waited after no pompe and reverence** he expected no ceremony or (exaggerated) respect

528 **Ne maked him a spiced conscience** was not too demanding in dealing with his flock

529 **loore** teaching

The Host accuses the Parson later of being a Lollard. Lollards held unorthodox religious views and objected to the wealth of the church – the term Lollard was contemptuous. The picture given here is of a pious and orthodox man whose life shows nothing but exemplary priestly devotion. After some general musings on the ill effects of sinful priests on the lives of their parishioners, Chaucer makes a strong attack on clerical corruption and weakness by pointing out that the Parson does not share these faults.

For if a preest be foul, on whom we truste,
No wonder is a lewed man to ruste;
And shame it is, if a prest take keep,   505
A shiten shepherde and a clene sheep.
Wel oghte a preest ensample for to yive,
By his clennesse, how that his sheep sholde live.
He sette nat his benefice to hire
And leet his sheep encombred in the mire   510
And ran to Londoun unto Seinte Poules
To seken him a chaunterie for soules,
Or with a bretherhed to been withholde;
But dwelte at hoom, and kepte wel his folde,
So that the wolf ne made it nat miscarie;   515
He was a shepherde and noght a mercenarie.
And though he hooly were and vertuous,
He was to sinful men nat despitous,
Ne of his speche daungerous ne digne,
But in his teching discreet and benigne.   520
To drawen folk to hevene by fairnesse,
By good ensample, this was his bisynesse.
But it were any persone obstinat,
What so he were, of heigh or lough estat,
Him wolde he snibben sharply for the nonis.   525
A bettre preest I trowe that nowher noon is.
He waited after no pompe and reverence,
Ne maked him a spiced conscience,
But Cristes loore and his apostles twelve
He taughte, but first he folwed it himselve.   530

- Read aloud lines 531–7. Can you hear a change in the language at any point, in the kind of words used and in the content? If so, can you account for it?
- Make a list of both the Plowman's worldly and religious virtues.
- Why do you think Chaucer includes no physical description of the Plowman?
- What motives do you think the Plowman might have for being on the pilgrimage?

532 **ylad of dong ful many a fother** had carried many a load of manure

533 **swinkere** worker, labourer

536 **thogh him gamed or smerte** in all circumstances [*literally:* whether in pleasure or pain]

537 **And thanne his neighebor right as himselve** and after [God] he loved his neighbour as himself. [See the first Commandment.]

538 **thresshe, and therto dike and delve** thresh and then (also) construct ditches and dig

539 **povre wight** poor person

540 **withouten hire** without payment [Compare many of the professional people and clerics in the company.]

541 **tithes** taxes of 10 per cent of all he produced, paid to support the Church

542 **Bothe of his propre swink and his catel** he paid by his own labour [on the priest's land] and in kind

543 **In a tabard he rood upon a mere** dressed in a humble tunic [as befitted his rank and unworldly outlook], he rode on a mare [regarded as a humble steed]

He wolde thresshe, and therto dike and delve,
... for every povre wight'

The Plowman is the Parson's brother, literally and figuratively, with the same selfless devotion to Christ. He is the lowest ranking pilgrim but is described with deep respect. Estates satire (see pages 93–4) often saw workers as lazy, and demanding ever higher wages in the labour shortage following the Black Death, but Chaucer's Plowman (a free, skilled land worker who owned some property) is a man whose humble work glorifies God and produces food to support other people. His faith, dignity and charity make him an ideal Christian.

With him ther was a Plowman, was his brother,
That hadde ylad of dong ful many a fother;
A trewe swinkere and a good was he,
Livinge in pees and parfit charitee.
God loved he best with al his hoole herte   535
At alle times, thogh him gamed or smerte,
And thanne his neighebor right as himselve.
He wolde thresshe, and therto dike and delve,
For Cristes sake, for every povre wight,
Withouten hire, if it lay in his might.   540
His tithes paide he ful faire and wel,
Bothe of his propre swink and his catel.
In a tabard he rood upon a mere.

- Read aloud lines 547–59. How would you describe the language in these lines, in tone and in meaning? How does it compare with the language used to describe the Plowman?
- Look at the similes used by Chaucer to describe the Miller. What do these suggest about his appearance, behaviour and character? (A large mouth in Chaucer's time was conventionally used to suggest greed, and red hair was thought of as a sign of hot temper. It still is.)
- What comparisons can you draw between the services provided to their clients by, for example, the Doctor or the Sergeant of the Law, and the services provided by the Miller?
- What could be the Miller's reason for going on the pilgrimage?

547   **a stout carl** a strongly built churl [low-born type]

       for the nones extremely

548   **big ... of brawn** well muscled

549   **over al ther he cam** wherever he went

550   **the ram** the prize for wrestling

551   **knarre** rough type

552   **he nolde heve of harre** that he would not pull from its hinges

556   **the cop right** right on the top

558   **eris** ears

559   **nosethirles** nostrils

560   **bokeler** small round shield

561   **forneys** furnace

562   **janglere and goliardeys** a loudmouth and a buffoon or clown

563   **and that** [his talk]

564   **tollen thries** take his toll three times over [take a proportion of everyone's corn as payment for grinding it, and then steal twice as much again]

565   **And yet he hadde a thombe of gold, pardee** he had a thumb of gold, by God [This proverb refers to the thumb millers used to examine corn, and which therefore brought them their profit. Honest millers were said to have a thumb of gold, but honest millers and gold thumbs are equally impossible.]

Perhaps aware that his list might be getting too long for his listeners, Chaucer assures us that there are only five more pilgrims to come, apart from himself. He then introduces the Miller: a grossly physical, strong and brutal man, repulsive in appearance and manners. Millers had great power over people at harvest time, and had a reputation for dishonesty, sharp practice and profiteering.

Ther was also a Reve, and a Millere,
A Somnour, and a Pardoner also,   545
A Maunciple, and myself—ther were namo.
The Millere was a stout carl for the nones;
Ful big he was of brawn, and eek of bones.
That proved wel, for over al ther he cam,
At wrastlinge he wolde have alwey the ram.   550
He was short-sholdred, brood, a thikke knarre;
Ther was no dore that he nolde heve of harre,
Or breke it at a renning with his heed.
His berd as any sowe or fox was reed,
And therto brood, as though it were a spade.   555
Upon the cop right of his nose he hade
A werte, and theron stood a toft of heris,
Reed as the brustles of a sowes eris;
His nosethirles blake were and wide.
A swerd and bokeler bar he by his side.   560
His mouth as greet was as a greet forneys.
He was a janglere and a goliardeys,
And that was moost of sinne and harlotries.
Wel koude he stelen corn and tollen thries;
And yet he hadde a thombe of gold, pardee.   565
A whit cote and a blew hood wered he.
A baggepipe wel koude he blowe and sowne,
And therwithal he broghte us out of towne.

- Consider lines 569–74, particularly the verbs. What impression do they give you of the Manciple's character?
- Lines 578–88 are all one sentence. What impression do they give of the Manciple and of the lawyers who were his employers, and how do they do this?
- In the light of lines 578–89, what tone would you think suitable for lines 575–7?
- Look back at line 569. What is suggested to you by the word 'gentil'?
- Line 588 suggests a secret life. Write a day's diary of activities and events that might reveal this aspect of the Manciple's life.

569	temple [either the Middle Temple or the Inner Temple, two of the Inns of Court in London]
570	achatours purchasers, caterers
571	byinge of vitaille buying provisions
572	paide or took by taille paid cash or took on credit ['taille' means 'tally']
573	waited so in his achaat waited until the right time to buy
574	ay biforn and in good staat always ahead of the game and with sound reserves
576	lewed uneducated
578	maistres the lawyers he served
	mo than thries ten more than thirty
579	expert and curious highly skilled and painstaking
581	stiwardes of rente and lond [A lord's steward ran his estate, hiring and firing and controlling the budget.]
583	live by his propre good to live within his (the lord's) income
584	wood mad
585	live as scarsly as him list desire live as economically as he (the lord) wanted to
586	to helpen al a shire to help anyone [literally: to help all the inhabitants of a county]
588	sette hir alle cappe fooled them all

The Manciple looks after the provisions and supplies of one of the Inns of Court, a building housing a group of lawyers who live and eat communally. He is very good at his job, and is discreet to the point of invisibility. Chaucer tells us nothing of his appearance or his personality, and nothing directly of his moral nature. We are told no details of his work, which was similar to that of the Reeve. This Manciple's lack of education might suggest he has carved out his own position. Perhaps his physical invisibility arises from his indeterminate status, as well as from his particular kind of ability.

A gentil Maunciple was ther of a temple,
Of which achatours mighte take exemple   570
For to be wise in byinge of vitaille;
For wheither that he paide or took by taille,
Algate he waited so in his achaat
That he was ay biforn and in good staat.
Now is nat that of God a ful fair grace   575
That swich a lewed mannes wit shal pace
The wisdom of an heep of lerned men?
Of maistres hadde he mo than thries ten,
That weren of lawe expert and curious,
Of which ther were a duszeyne in that hous   580
Worthy to been stiwardes of rente and lond
Of any lord that is in Engelond,
To make him live by his propre good
In honour dettelees (but if he were wood),
Or live as scarsly as him list desire;   585
And able for to helpen al a shire
In any caas that mighte falle or happe;
And yet this Manciple sette hir aller cappe.

- There are plenty of details in the description of the Reeve. What physical impression of him do you receive from lines 587–94?
- Why should the bailiff, the 'hierde' and other 'hine' dread this Reeve 'as of the deeth' (lines 605–7)?

590	**ny** close, short	601	**governinge** control
592	**dokked lyk a preest** cut short like a priest [A priest would wear the tonsure, a patch of hair shaved on the head, to show his office and status.]	602	**by his covenant yaf the rekeninge** according to his contract, accounted to his master
		604	**bringe him in arrerage** accuse him of leaving bills unpaid when they were due
595	**gerner and a binne** granary and corn-bin	605	**hierde** herdsman
596	**noon auditour koude on him winne** no auditor (accountant) could catch him out (in an error in his accounts)		**hine** labourer
		607	**That he ne knew his sleighte and his covine** whose crafty tricks and deceit he did not know
599	**neet** cattle		
600	**swyn** pigs	607	**adrad** terrified
	stoor stock		

The Reeve serves a landowner in the country by managing his estates, tenants and workers. He controls his lord's estate completely, a task usually given to more than one official. His physical build fits the choleric type, made thin and sinewy by the sheer heat of his nature, but there is no sign of the quick temper of the choleric man.

   The Reve was a sclendre colerik man.
His berd was shave as ny as ever he kan;   590
His heer was by his eris ful round yshorn;
His top was dokked lyk a preest biforn.
Ful longe were his legges and ful lene,
Ylik a staf, ther was no calf ysene.
Wel koude he kepe a gerner and a binne;   595
Ther was noon auditour koude on him winne.
Wel wiste he by the droghte and by the reyn
The yeldinge of his seed and of his greyn.
His lordes sheep, his neet, his dayerie,
His swyn, his hors, his stoor, and his pultrie   600
Was hoolly in this Reves governinge,
And by his covenant yaf the rekeninge,
Syn that his lord was twenty yeer of age.
Ther koude no man bringe him in arrerage.
Ther nas baillif, ne hierde, nor oother hine,   605
That he ne knew his sleighte and his covine;
They were adrad of him as of the deeth.

- What further impression of the Reeve's appearance do you receive from lines 617–24?
- Chaucer says little to the Reeve's disadvantage but the description is not wholeheartedly approving of him. What impression do you receive of the Reeve's character, and how is that conveyed?
- Which two or three adjectives would you choose to describe the Reeve? Compare the result with a partner and explain your choice.

608   **woning** house, dwelling

610   **He koude bettre than his lord purchace** he could buy property more skilfully, or more cheaply, than his lord

611   **Ful riche he was astored prively** he had his own wealth hidden away

612   **subtilly** cleverly

613   **To yeve and lene him of his owene good** to give and lend him his (his lord's) own property

614   **yet** also

615   **myster** a trade [A trade regulated by those who practised it was called a mystery, the word suggesting that some of the trade's skills and knowledge had to be restricted in the interests of its practitioners.]

616   **wrighte** craftsman

617   **stot** stallion

618   **pomely** dappled

619   **surcote of pers** a bluish-grey overcoat

621   **Northfolk** [People from Norfolk had something of a reputation for avarice.]

622   **clepen** call

623   **Tukked he was as is a frere** (his coat) tucked up into his belt like a friar's (when riding)

624   **rood the hindreste of oure route** always rode at the rear of our group [This might have been partly because of his character, and partly to keep as far away as possible from the Miller who led the way. A miller and reeve would be likely to view each other suspiciously.]

There is a suggestion that the Reeve has the cunning and the tendency to fraudulence that was sometimes associated with the choleric type, and yet not much detail is given of his dishonesty. He had been a carpenter when younger, and Chaucer adds a number of details about his background in Norfolk.

His woning was ful faire upon an heeth;
With grene trees yshadwed was his place.
He koude bettre than his lord purchace.   610
Ful riche he was astored prively:
His lord wel koude he plesen subtilly,
To yeve and lene him of his owene good,
And have a thank, and yet a cote and hood.
In youthe he hadde lerned a good myster;   615
He was a wel good wrighte, a carpenter.
This Reve sat upon a ful good stot,
That was al pomely grey and highte Scot.
A long surcote of pers upon he hade,
And by his side he baar a rusty blade.   620
Of Northfolk was this Reve of which I telle,
Biside a toun men clepen Baldeswelle.
Tukked he was as is a frere aboute,
And evere he rood the hindreste of oure route.

The Summoner is an official who summons people to come before church courts. These separate courts were set up to deal with offending clergy, who could not be brought before the ordinary courts for any crime except treason. The church courts also tried lay people for moral offences such as adultery, and for non-payment of tithes and many other sins or crimes.

• The Summoner's description tells of a physically disgusting man. What do we also learn of his character?

626 **cherubinnes** cherubs [An ironical comparison, as cherubs are heavenly creatures – they were, however, customarily drawn with bright red faces.]

627 **saucefleem** pimply [caused by an excess of salty phlegm in the diet. The pimples were thought to be a symptom of leprosy. The sufferer was supposed to abstain from sexual activity and all highly seasoned food. See lines 628 and 636.]

narwe narrow

628 **sparwe** sparrow [long associated with lechery]

629 **scalled browes blake and piled berd** scaly black brows and a beard that was dropping out

630 **visage** face
aferd afraid

631-3 **quik-silver, litarge ... Ne oinement** mercury, protoxide of lead, sulphur, borax, white lead, oil of tartar and caustic ointment based on arsenic [all thought to be medicines for the Summoner's diseases]

634 **whelkes** pustules

636 **garleek, oynons, and eek lekes** [The Summoner's diet is not only medically undesirable, but also socially.]

640 **speke no word but Latin** [It was a common idea that people gabbled in Latin when drunk.]

643 **he herd it al the day** [in the church court where he was employed]

644–5 **And eek ye ... kan the pope** and you know as well as I do that a jay can call out 'Walter' as well as the pope can [Jays, like jackdaws, can be taught to imitate human speech.]

646 **But whoso koude ... him grope** but if anyone tested him further (in Latin)

648 *Questio quid iuris?* the question is, which part of the law? [The Summoner would have heard this at some stage in his work.]

649 **a gentil harlot** a gentlemanly villain [Harlot came to mean 'prostitute' in the fifteenth century.]

The Summoner is a repulsive man, with many untreatable physical afflictions; he is also addicted to the bottle.

A Somonour was ther with us in that place,   625
That hadde a fyr-reed cherubinnes face,
For saucefleem he was, with eyen narwe.
As hoot he was and lecherous as a sparwe,
With scalled browes blake and piled berd.
Of his visage children were aferd.   630
Ther nas quik-silver, litarge, ne brimstoon,
Boras, ceruce, ne oille of tartre noon;
Ne oinement that wolde clense and bite,
That him mighte helpen of his whelkes white,
Nor of the knobbes sittinge on his chekes.   635
Wel loved he garleek, oynons, and eek lekes,
And for to drinken strong wyn, reed as blood;
Thanne wolde he speke and crie as he were wood.
And whan that he wel dronken hadde the wyn,
Thanne wolde he speke no word but Latin.   640
A fewe termes hadde he, two or thre,
That he had lerned out of som decree—
No wonder is, he herde it al the day;
And eek ye knowen wel how that a jay
Kan clepen 'Watte' as wel as kan the pope.   645
But whoso koude in oother thing him grope,
Thanne hadde he spent al his philosophie;
Ay '*Questio quid iuris*' wolde he crie.
He was a gentil harlot and a kinde;
A bettre felawe sholde men noght finde.   650

- What do lines 669–70 suggest to you about the Summoner's character?
- Chaucer is describing a corrupt individual. How far would you say he is also criticising social and religious structures?

651–3 **He wolde suffre … twelf month** for two pints of wine he would let a man keep a mistress for a whole year [without informing on him to the church courts]

654 **prively** secretly

pulle pluck, or draw out the guts [The line suggests that he too sought out prostitutes.]

655 **owher** anywhere

656 **have noon awe** not to fear

657 **the ercedekenes curs** the archdeacon's condemnation [Excommunication could be the penalty for adultery. The bishop or the archdeacon presided in the church courts.]

658–9 **But if a mannes … ypunissed be** unless the man's soul were kept in his purse, for it is only in his purse that he need be punished

660 **'Purs is …' seyde he** an offender suffered financially rather than being condemned to suffer in hell

661 **lied right in dede** told a complete lie

662 **cursing** excommunication, damnation

663 **slee** damn, kill

assoilling absolution

664 **war him** be careful to avoid

Significavit writ threatening imprisonment ['Significavit' was the first word of the writ authorising imprisonment of a person excommunicated for offences such as non-payment of tithes or fornication.]

665–6 **In daunger hadde … of the diocise** he had complete control, in his own way, of the young men and women of the diocese ['Girls' at that stage meant young people of both sexes.]

667 **hir conseil** their secrets

was al hir reed was adviser or counsellor to them all

669 **ale-stake** a bush set up on a stake outside an ale-house to indicate to an illiterate population that drink was available there

670 **A bokeleer … cake** he had made himself a shield out of a large cake or loaf

The list of offences that could lead to an appearance before the church courts was long and could almost be applied to any action. There were thus many opportunities for corruption, about which the Summoner boasts. He is running a protection racket: the poor found it better to pay him a bribe to avoid an accusation, rather than risk going to court and being given an even larger fine. Failure to pay within a month meant excommunication and prison until payment was made. By taking bribes, the Summoner was encouraging the offences his post was designed to stop, and was profiting from them.

He wolde suffre for a quart of wyn
A good felawe to have his concubyn
A twelf month, and excuse him atte fulle;
Ful prively a finch eek koude he pulle.
And if he foond owher a good felawe,   655
He wolde techen him to have noon awe
In swich caas of the ercedekenes curs,
But if a mannes soule were in his purs;
For in his purs he sholde ypunisshed be.
'Purs is the ercedekenes helle,' seyde he.   660
But wel I woot he lied right in dede;
Of cursing oghte ech gilty man him drede,
For curs wol slee right as assoilling savith,
And also war him of a *Significavit.*
In daunger hadde he at his owene gise   665
The yonge girles of the diocise,
And knew hir conseil, and was al hir reed.
A gerland hadde he set upon his heed
As greet as it were for an ale-stake.
A bokeleer hadde he maad him of a cake.   670

The Summoner as depicted in the Ellesmere manuscript: 'A gerland hadde he set upon his heed'

By buying a pardon people could build up a kind of spiritual bank balance to set against their sins, provided they then confessed them to a priest and were absolved. Many people set themselves up as fraudulent Pardoners, with no authority from the church, and were therefore criminals. Pardoners also preached and sold relics, another source of fraud and corruption in religious life.

• The Pardoner has many unpleasant aspects. Draw up lists of those things that are a matter of his choice and those he cannot help.

672 **Of Rouncivale** from the hostel of St Mary Roncevall near Charing Cross in London [known as a foundation much involved with Pardoners]

compeer companion

675 **bar to him a stif burdoun** sung the bass part loudly. [As this is a love song there is a suggestion in this phrase of a homosexual relationship between the Summoner and the Pardoner.]

676 **trompe** trumpet

678 **strike of flex** hank of flax [dry and lifeless]

679 **ounces** small gatherings, bunches, rats' tails [Long hair was forbidden to clerics, suggesting this Pardoner was either not officially sanctioned, or did not care about the rules.]

681 **colpons** sections

682 **for jolitee** for the sake of his appearance

684 **al of the newe jet** in the very latest fashion

685 **Dischevelee ...bare** with his hair all dishevelled, he rode bareheaded except for his skull cap

686 **Swiche glaringe ... an hare** [Glaring eyes were thought of as the mark of a libertine, and the hare was spoken of as sleeping with open eyes. It was also considered a hermaphrodite.]

687 **vernicle** a medal with the representation of Veronica's veil, with which she wiped Christ's face when he was carrying his cross [It was a sign of having made a pilgrimage to Rome. 'Vernicle' is a diminutive of 'Veronica'.]

689 **bretful** brimful

The Pardoner is another monster of corruption, a suitable friend for the Summoner, presented in terms of disgust and contempt for his spiritual sterility, fraud and avarice. He lives by selling pardons, one of the most bitterly criticised corruptions of religious life in the fourteenth century.

With him ther rood a gentil Pardoner
Of Rouncivale, his freend and his compeer,
That streight was comen fro the court of Rome.
Ful loude he soong 'Com hider, love, to me!'
This Somonour bar to him a stif burdoun;   675
Was nevere trompe of half so greet a soun.
This Pardoner hadde heer as yelow as wex,
But smothe it heeng his lokkes that he hadde,
By ounces henge as dooth a strike of flex;
And therwith he his shuldres overspradde;   680
But thinne it lay, by colpons oon and oon.
But hood, for jolitee, wered he noon,
For it was trussed up in his walet.
Him thoughte he rood al of the newe jet;
Dischevelee, save his cappe, he rood al bare.   685
Swiche glaringe eyen hadde he as an hare.
A vernicle hadde he sowed upon his cappe.
His walet lay biforn him in his lappe,
Bretful of pardoun, comen from Rome al hoot.

- Compare the way Chaucer handles his description of the Pardoner with that of the Prioress (lines 118–164).
- The Pardoner's wrongdoing is described mercilessly. What is the effect of the description in lines 709–16?

690 **as smal as hath a goot** as weak as a goat's [thin and high]

691 **ne nevere sholde have** nor ever would have [he never would become an adult man]

692 **late** recently, newly

694 **fro Berwik into Ware** from Berwick to Ware [from the one end of the country to the other]

696 **male** pouch, luggage
pilwe-beer pillow case

698 **gobet of the seil** piece of the sail

700 **til Jhesu Crist him hente** till Jesus Christe took him (into the boat) [For the episode of walking on the water read St Matthew's Gospel, chapter 6.]

701 **crois of latoun ful of stones** a brass cross [Latoun is an alloy of tin and copper that looks like gold but is base metal. The stones or gems are presumably also false.]

704 **person** parson
upon land in the country

706 **gat in monthes tweye** received in two months

707 **feyned** pretended, false

708 **made the person and the peple his apes** made fools of the parson and the people (congregation)

709 **atte laste** finally

710 **noble ecclesiaste** a fine cleric

711 **lessoun or a storie** the readings from the Bible that take place during mass

712 **alderbest** best of all
offertorie that part of the mass, sung by priest and people, during which they made their offering

714 **affile** smooth

716 **murierly** more merrily

The Pardoner's ambiguous sexuality is suggested, before a list is given of the stock of relics he has for sale. His financial success is considerable, perhaps as a result of his great rhetorical skill in the pulpit.

A voys he hadde as smal as hath a goot.   690
No berd hadde he, ne nevere sholde have;
As smothe it was as it were late shave.
I trowe he were a gelding or a mare.
But of his craft, fro Berwik into Ware,
Ne was ther swich another pardoner.   695
For in his male he hadde a pilwe-beer,
Which that he seyde was Oure Lady veil:
He seyde he hadde a gobet of the seil
That Seint Peter hadde, whan that he wente
Upon the see, til Jhesu Crist him hente.   700
He hadde a crois of latoun ful of stones,
And in a glas he hadde pigges bones.
But with thise relikes, whan that he fond
A povre person dwellinge upon lond,
Upon a day he gat him moore moneye   705
Than that the person gat in monthes tweye;
And thus, with feyned flaterie and japes,
He made the person and the peple his apes.
But trewely to tellen atte laste,
He was in chirche a noble ecclesiaste.   710
Wel koude he rede a lessoun or a storie,
But alderbest he song an offertorie;
For wel he wiste, whan that song was songe,
He moste preche and wel affile his tonge
To winne silver, as he ful wel koude;   715
Therefore he song the murierly and loude.

- What impression of the age of Chaucer have you received from his description of the pilgrims?
- In line 746 Chaucer admits he has not kept to the accepted order of social rank in describing his pilgrims, as was the literary convention of the time. Look back over the order and the grouping of the descriptions, and say what you think the effects of this are. What, for instance is the effect of placing the first three pilgrims together, and of placing the Summoner and the Pardoner at the end?
- Although he is talking about lewd language and about actions that will arise in some of the Tales, Chaucer is here raising the question of how far art (poetry) can be truth. Read this section through again, and work out his oblique comments on the matter.

717 **soothly, in a clause** truthfully and briefly

721 **the Belle** another tavern [perhaps mentioned to add credibility]

723 **baren us that ilke night** behaved that same night

724 **alight** arrived

725 **viage** journey

728 **That ye n'arette it nat** so that you should not attribute it to

730 **cheere** behaviour

731 **Ne thogh I speke hir wordes proprely** even though I report their words exactly (as they said them) [He will show them through their own words, even if these are not always polite or respectable.]

733 **telle a tale after a man** tell a tale as if he were that man

734 **moot reherce** must repeat

as ny as exactly

735 **Everich a word, if it be in his charge** every single word, if it lies in his power; if it is his responsibility

736 **al speke he** even if he speaks

large directly, freely

738 **or feyne thing** or make something up (that is more acceptable)

740 **He moot ... as another** he must say one kind of word [foul language] as the other [respectable language]

741 **spak hymself ful brode** expressed himself broadly or plainly

742 **woot** know

no vileynie is it it [holy writ] is not improper

744 **The wordes moote ... the dede** the words must be closely related to the deed [This is a quotation from Plato's *Timaeus* which is at odds with much of what has been said in The General Prologue, where words are often used to deceive, or to conceal the nature of a deed.]

746 **al** although

in hir degree in their proper social ranking

748 **ye may well understonde** as you will have gathered [Chaucer-the-narrator presents himself in *The Canterbury Tales* as genial, unworldly and innocent.]

Chaucer has fulfilled his intention (lines 35–41) of telling the 'condicioun', 'degree' and 'array' of each of his 29 pilgrims. He apologises in advance for the earthy thoughts and language of some of the Tales that follow. This apology is partly a literary convention of the time, but Chaucer seems almost to be giving a warning that words are not always what they seem to be.

Now have I toold you soothly, in a clause,
Th'estaat, th'array, the nombre, and eek the cause
Why that assembled was this compaignie
In Southwerk at this gentil hostelrie   720
That highte the Tabard, faste by the Belle.
But now is time to yow for to telle
How that we baren us that ilke night,
Whan we were in that hostelrie alight;
And after wol I telle of our viage   725
And al the remenaunt of oure pilgrimage.
But first I pray yow, of your curteisie,
That ye n'arette it nat my vileynie,
Thogh that I pleynly speke in this mateere,
To telle yow hir wordes and hir cheere,   730
Ne thogh I speke hir wordes proprely.
For this ye knowen al so wel as I,
Whoso shal telle a tale after a man,
He moot reherce as ny as evere he kan
Everich a word, if it be in his charge,   735
Al speke he never so rudeliche and large,
Or ellis he moot telle his tale untrewe,
Or feyne thing, or finde wordes newe.
He may nat spare, althogh he were his brother;
He moot as wel seye o word as another.   740
Crist spak hymself ful brode in hooly writ,
And wel ye woot no vileynie is it.
Eek Plato seith, whoso that kan him rede,
The wordes moote be cosin to the dede.
Also I prey yow to foryeve it me,   745
Al have I nat set folk in hir degree
Heere in this tale, as that they sholde stonde.
My wit is short, ye may wel understonde.

• The pilgrims, having eaten and drunk very well, have become a company or fellowship. What does the Host do to help bring this about?

749 **us everichon** every one of us

750 **to the soper sette he us** he sat us down to supper

751 **vitaille at the beste** the very best food

752 **wel to drinke us leste** we were glad to drink

753 **semely** impressive

754 **a marchal in an halle** a master of ceremonies, supervising the proper serving of the meal in an important house

755 **eyen stepe** large, bright eyes

756 **burgeys** a freeman or citizen

 Chepe Cheapside, a street in the City of London [The suggestion is that even though an outsider from across the river, he was the equal of anyone in the metropolis. 'Cheap' means to sell, and is the origin of the modern word meaning 'not expensive'.]

758 **And of manhod ... naught** lacked nothing at all of the qualities proper to manhood

760 **pleyen he bigan** began to joke with the company

762 **rekeninges** bills [first things first]

763 **lordinges** 'Sirs' [equivalent to today's 'Ladies and gentlemen']

767 **Atones in this herberwe** together in this inn

For the first time since line 34 the narrative of The General Prologue is resumed. The Host (named in the Cook's Prologue as Harry Bailly, a man who actually lived in Southwark at the time) serves a splendid meal, well lubricated with wine. Once all bills have been settled, he declares that the group gathered under his roof that night is the merriest he has seen that year.

   Greet chiere made oure Hoost us everichon,
And to the soper sette he us anon.   750
He served us with vitaille at the beste;
Strong was the wyn, and wel to drinke us leste.
A semely man Oure Hooste was withalle
For to han been a marchal in an halle.
A large man he was with eyen stepe—   755
A fairer burgeys is ther noon in Chepe—
Boold of his speche, and wys, and wel ytaught,
And of manhod him lakkede right naught.
Eek therto he was right a mirie man,
And after soper pleyen he bigan,   760
And spak of mirthe amonges othere thinges,
Whan that we hadde maad oure rekeninges,
And seyde thus: 'Now, lordinges, trewely,
Ye been to me right welcome, hertely;
For by my trouthe, if that I shal nat lie,   765
I saugh nat this yeer so mirie a compaignie
Atones in this herberwe as is now.

- What is the effect of putting the paying of bills just before the Host's wish that the pilgrims might be rewarded by St Thomas?
- How would you decribe the Host's character as it is revealed in this section?

768–9 **Fain wolde ... now bithoght** I would like to entertain you, if I knew how and I have just thought of a way of doing so

770 **To doon yow ese** to give you pleasure

771 **God yow speede** may God speed your journey

772 **quite yow youre meede** reward you, give you your deserts [*literally:* match or pay your reward]

774 **Ye shapen ... to pleye** you are planning to tell tales and amuse yourselves

777 **disport** amusement

778 **erst** earlier

779 **And if yow ... oon assent** and if you approve unanimously

780 **stonden at my juggement** accept my judgment or decision

783 **fader** father's

784 **But ye me mirie ... myn heed!** if you don't enjoy yourselves, I will give you my head!

The Host is looking for a way to amuse the pilgrims. He suggests that if they put themselves in his hands, they will find his proposal amusing – or else he will answer for it with his own head. And it will cost them nothing.

Fain wolde I doon yow mirthe, wiste I how.
And of a mirthe I am right now bithoght,
To doon yow ese, and it shal coste noght.   770
   Ye goon to Caunterbury—God yow speede,
The blisful martir quite yow youre meede!
And wel I woot, as ye goon by the weye,
Ye shapen yow to talen and to pleye;
For trewely, confort ne mirthe is noon   775
To ride by the weye doumb as a stoon;
And therfore wol I maken yow disport,
As I seyde erst, and doon yow som confort.
And if yow liketh alle by oon assent
For to stonden at my juggement,   780
And for to weken as I shal yow seye,
To-morwe, whan ye riden by the weye,
Now, by my fader soule that is deed,
But ye be mirie, I wol yeve yow myn heed!
Hoold up youre hondes, withouten moore speche.'   785

- How would you describe the Host's language as he puts his proposal forward?
- Pilgrimages were generally cheerful occasions, but how would you describe the journey that the Host is proposing?

786   **conseil** decision
      seche seek

787   **to make it wys** to think about it, raise objections

788   **withouten moore avys** without further discussion; without more ado

789   **voirdit** verdict
      as him leste as he wished

790   **herkneth for the beste** listen for your own advantage (for the best thing to do)

791   **taak it nought ... in desdeyn** do not disdain it; do not turn you noses up at it

793   **to shorte with** to shorten

794   **tweye** two

796   **othere two** another two

797   **Of aventures ... bifalle** of stories that happened in past times

798   **bereth him best** does best; tells the best story

799   **in this caas** in this affair or competition

800   **sentence** meaning
      solaas pleasure [*literally:* solace or comfort]

801   **at oure aller cost** paid for by all of us, or by the rest of us

805   **goodly** gladly

806   **Right at myn ... youre gide** I will not charge for my services as master of ceremonies on the pilgrimage

807   **withseye** contradict, argue with

808   **by the weye** on the road

809   **vouche sauf** agree [a very polite form]

810   **anon** at once, immediately

811   **I wol erly shape me therfore** I will get myself ready for it early (the next morning)

The Host, having got the company's attention and agreement, now reveals what they have agreed to – a competition in story-telling, with himself as judge, and a dinner in his own inn as the prize, paid for by the rest of the company.

Oure conseil was nat longe for to seche.
Us thoughte it was noght worth to make it wys,
And graunted him withouten moore avys,
And bad him seye his voirdit as him leste.
'Lordinges,' quod he, 'now herkneth for the beste;   790
But taak it nought, I prey yow, in desdeyn.
This is the point, to speken short and pleyn,
That ech of yow, to shorte with oure weye,
In this viage shal telle tales tweye
To Caunterbury-ward, I mene it so,   795
And homward he shal tellen othere two,
Of aventures that whilom han bifalle.
And which of yow that bereth him best of alle,
That is to seyn, that telleth in this caas
Tales of best sentence and moost solaas,   800
Shal have a soper at oure aller cost
Heere in this place, sittinge by this post,
Whan that we come again fro Caunterbury.
And for to make yow the moore mury,
I wol myselven goodly with yow ride,   805
Right at myn owene cost, and be youre gide;
And whoso wole my juggement withseye
Shal paye al that we spenden by the weye.
And if ye vouche sauf that it be so,
Tel me anon, withouten wordes mo,   810
And I wol erly shape me therfore.'

• Some of the pilgrims later test the Host's patience and determination with quarrels and interruptions. Read the sentence in lines 812–20. What mood does its tone and content suggest about the party?

812	**oure othes sworn** our agreement pledged ['We' is understood here, as it is in line 813 – '(we) preyden'.]
816	**reportour** score keeper
818	**reuled been at his devys** ruled according to his plan or proposal
819	**in heigh and lough** in all things, in every respect
	oon one, single
820	**we been acorded to** we agreed to
821	**fet** fetched
822	**echon** each of us, all of us
823	**lenger taryinge** further delay
824	**amorwe** the next day
825	**roos** rose
	oure aller cok woke us all up [*literally*: cockerel for us all]
826	**gadrede** gathered
	togidre together

827	**a litel moore than paas** slightly faster than a (horse's) walk
828	**wateringe of Seint Thomas** a stream called after the saint [about two miles out of London]
829	**areste** pull up
831	**Ye woot youre ... recorde** you know your agreement and I remind you of it
832	**If even-song and morwe-song accorde** if what you said last night agrees with what you say this morning
834	**as ever mote I drinke** if ever I might drink [It carries the overtones of the modern expression 'So help me'.]
837	**Now draweth cut ... twinne** now draw lots before we set out any further

There is a general hearty agreement, as the company puts itself enthusiastically in the Host's hands. He repeats the main points of the agreement so that there should no mistake. The Host wakes them all early, and gets them under way. Two miles outside London, they halt to water the horses, and the Host reminds them yet again, in polite but firm terms, of their agreement.

This thing was graunted, and oure othes swore
With ful glad herte, and preyden him also
That he wolde vouche sauf for to do so,
And that he wolde been oure governour,   815
And of oure tales juge and reportour,
And sette a soper at a certeyn prys,
And we wol reuled been at his devys
In heigh and lough; and thus by oon assent
We been acorded to his juggement.   820
And therupon the wyn was fet anon;
We dronken, and to reste wente echon,
Withouten any lenger taryinge.
Amorwe, whan that day bigan to springe,
Up roos oure Hoost, and was oure aller cok,   825
And gadrede us togidre alle in a flok,
And forth we riden a litel moore than paas
Unto the wateringe of Seint Thomas;
And there oure Hoost bigan his hors areste
And seyde, 'Lordinges, herkneth, if yow leste.   830
Ye woot youre foreward, and I it yow recorde.
If even-song and morwe-song accorde,
Lat se now who shal telle the firste tale.
As evere mote I drinke wyn or ale,
Whoso be rebel to my juggement   835
Shal paye for al that by the wey is spent.
Now draweth cut, er that we ferrer twinne;
He which that hath the shorteste shal biginne.

- How would you describe the language and action in lines 839–43?
- What reasons do you think the pilgrims might have for feeling pleased that the Knight is to tell the first tale?
- Look at the Knight's words as he accepts the honour of going first. What is his approach to his story?

840 **for that is myn accord** for that is the agreement that you made with me

842 **lat be youre shamefastnesse** forget your shyness

843 **ne studieth noght** don't examine it

ley hond to, every man everyone take a straw

846 **by aventure, or sort, or cas** by chance

847 **the cut fil to the Knight** the winning straw was drawn by the Knight [*literally*: the cut fell to the Knight]

849 **as was resoun** as was fair or reasonable [A reminder that Chaucer had said (line 37) that it was according to reason that he should describe all the pilgrims. He is allowing the Knight to go first, as if to make up for failing to keep to the ranking of the pilgrims during The General Prologue.]

850 **By foreward and by composicioun** according to the agreement and arrangement

855 **sin** since

856 **a Goddes name** in God's name

857 **herkneth** hear, listen to [the polite form]

The Host asks the Knight to draw first and, by chance, the Knight draws the winning straw,
which pleases everyone else. He suggests they move on, and prepares to tell his tale.

Sire Knight,' quod he, 'my maister and my lord,
Now draweth cut, for that is myn accord.   840
Cometh neer,' quod he, 'my lady Prioresse.
And ye, sire Clerk, lat be youre shamefastnesse,
Ne studieth noght; ley hond to, every man!'
Anon to drawen every wight bigan,
And shortly for to tellen as it was,   845
Were it by aventure, or sort, or cas,
The sothe is this, the cut fil to the Knight,
Of which ful blithe and glad was every wight,
And telle he moste his tale, as was resoun,
By foreward and by composicioun,   850
As ye han herd; what nedeth wordes mo?
And whan this goode man saugh that it was so,
As he that wys was and obedient
To kepe his foreward by his free assent,
He seyde, 'Sin I shal biginne the game,   855
What, welcome be the cut, a Goddes name!
Now lat us ride, and herkneth what I seye'.
And with that word we riden forth oure weye,
And he bigan with right a mirie cheere
His tale anon, and seyde as ye may heere.

Chaucer's pilgrims

In order of appearance:

The Knight	brave, devout and unassuming – the perfect gentleman
The Squire	in training to follow in the Knight, his father's, footsteps, a fine and fashionable young man, and madly in love
The Yeoman	the Knight's only servant, a skilled bowman and forester
The Prioress	a most ladylike head of a nunnery; she takes great pains with her appearance and manners; she loves animals. She is accompanied by another nun and three priests, the nun and one priest also telling tales
The Monk	fine and prosperous looking, well-mounted; he loves hunting
The Friar	cheerful and sociable, he is skilled at obtaining alms from those he visits, particularly the ladies
The Merchant	rather secretive; his main interest is commerce
The Clerk	thin and shabby, his passion is scholarship; he spends all he has on books
The Sergeant at Law	judge at the assize courts; skilled at making personal profit from his office; one of the few pilgrims about whom Chaucer says very little
The Franklin	wealthy and hospitable landowner and a JP; but not a member of the aristocracy
The Five Guildsmen	although they pursue different crafts or trades, they belong to the same social guild – rather self-important townsfolk
The Cook	brought along by the Guildsmen; although a versatile cook, Chaucer suggests his personal hygiene could be improved
The Shipman	weather-beaten master mariner

The Doctor of Physic finely dressed and a skilled medical practitioner; he is an expert in astrology and natural magic; he loves gold

The Wife of Bath skilled at weaving; her chief claim to fame is her five husbands

The Parson the only truly devout churchman in Chaucer's group; he avoids all the tricks unscrupulous clerics used to get rich, and spends his care and energy on his parishioners

The Ploughman the Parson's brother; like him, a simple, honest hard-working man

The Miller tough, ugly and a cheat

The Manciple responsible for organising the provisions for the lawyers in one of the Inns of Court – a plum job for a clever man

The Reeve unsociable, but able; the estate manager of a young nobleman

The Summoner an official of a church court; corrupt, lewd and offensive

The Pardoner another unpleasant churchman; he earns money by selling 'pardons' from Rome, and by letting simple folk see the fake holy relics he carries

The Host the genial landlord of 'The Tabard', who accompanies them on the pilgrimage, and organises the story-telling

Geoffrey Chaucer he depicts himself as rather shy and unassuming.

They are later joined by another story teller, **The Canon's Yeoman**, a servant whose tale betrays his master's obsessive interest in alchemy.

Chaucer's pilgrims, as depicted in a nineteenth century painting

Pilgrims and pilgrimages

Pilgrimages are journeys made to sacred places, usually as acts of religious devotion. They became increasingly popular during the twelfth and thirteen centuries, at the time when fear of threats to the Christian world from infidels and heathens from the east reached their height. The passion to defend and reaffirm the power of the Christian church manifested itself in Crusades to the Holy Land, and an upsurge in religious fervour. Shrines were established in many European countries in places of great religious significance. In England, Canterbury Cathedral was the site of the assassination of Archbishop Becket; Walsingham in Norfolk became a holy site of pilgrimage after visions of the Virgin Mary had been seen there. The great cathedral city of Cologne was another centre of pilgrimage, as was Compostela. Further afield, many pilgrims made the long journey to Jerusalem itself, available for visits from Christian pilgrims after the Emperor Frederick II had negotiated peace with the infidels, and had himself crowned king of the holy city.

Pilgrims (travelling in groups for companionship and safety) would travel to shrines at home and abroad to celebrate their devotion to the church, to seek pardon for their sins, and to ask favours of the saint whose relics were preserved in that place. The traditional image of a pilgrim is of one who travels humbly and simply, dressed in plain clothes, often on foot, carrying a staff. The emblem of a pilgrim is the scallop or cockle shell, worn on cap or hood. This was particularly the symbol of St James, patron saint of military crusaders, and the journey to his shrine in Compostela, northern Spain, was, and still is, one of the great pilgrim routes across Europe. The shells may originally have been real ones, but were later moulded in lead, as were most other pilgrim badges.

By the time Chaucer decided to use a group of pilgrims as a framework for his *Canterbury Tales,* reasons for pilgrimage had become less exclusively devotional. It was certainly a profitable business for enterprising people, as well as a popular pastime. The tourist industry began to take off. The Venetians offered a regular ferry service carrying travellers to and from the Holy Land. The monks of Cluny, the greatest religious house in France, ran a string of hotels along the entire route between their monastery and Compostela. Travel guides were produced, giving information about accommodation available along the route. One for Compostela contained useful Basque vocabulary, and a description of what to see in the cathedral. Horse traders did a healthy trade hiring out horses to pilgrims.

There was great competition for popular relics between the religious establishments, which sometimes led to rather obvious forgeries. At least two places, for instance, claimed to possess the head of John the Baptist. Pilgrims began to bring home their own souvenirs, and to house them in their local churches, like the fourteenth century traveller William Wey, who proudly deposited in his Wiltshire village church his maps, a reproduction of St Veronica's handkerchief, which he had rubbed on the pillars of 'the tempyl of Jerusalem', and a large number of stones picked up in sites around the Holy Land. His parish priest was presumably delighted. Badges and emblems made of lead were sold at shrines, and eagerly purchased as souvenirs by travellers – the cockle shell for St James, the palm tree from Jericho. At Canterbury it was possible to buy an assortment of badges – an image of the head of the saint, St Thomas riding a horse, a little bell, or a small ampulla [bottle] to hold sacred water. Permission was given from Rome for the local religious houses to obtain a licence to manufacture these.

Some of Chaucer's pilgrims seem to have genuinely devout reasons for visiting Canterbury: the Knight, for instance, has come straight from his military expeditions abroad, fighting for Christendom, and his simple coat is still stained from its contact with his coat of mail. On the other hand, the Wife of Bath, although an enthusiastic pilgrim, hardly seems to be travelling in a spirit of piety or devotion. She lists the places she has visited like a seasoned traveller determined to visit as many tourist attractions as possible. By using a pilgrimage as the frame on which to hang his stories and characterisations, Chaucer was able to point out the way in which attitudes and standards were changing and old values were being lost.

Geoffrey Chaucer

Geoffrey Chaucer

BIOGRAPHICAL NOTES

1340? The actual date of his birth is uncertain, but he was near 60 when he died. His father and grandfather were both vintners – wealthy London merchants, who supplied wines to the king's court.

Chaucer was introduced to court life in his teens. By the age of 16 he was employed in the service of the wife of the king's son, Lionel, later Duke of Clarence.

1359 He fought in France in the army of Edward III. He was captured and imprisoned, but released on payment of his ransom by the duke.

Chaucer was clearly valued by the king and other members of the royal family. In the **1360s** and **1370s** he was sent on diplomatic missions to France, Genoa, Florence and Lombardy.

1360s He married Philippa de Roet, a maid-in-waiting to Edward III's wife, Queen Philippa. His wife's half-sister was Katherine Swynford, third wife of John of Gaunt. The link with this powerful Duke of Lancaster was an important one; the duke was Chaucer's patron and in later life gave him a pension of £10 a year.

1368? Chaucer wrote *The Book of the Duchess*, a poem on the death of the Duchess Blanche, first wife of John of Gaunt.

1374 The position of Comptroller of Customs for the port of London was given to Chaucer, and in the same year the king granted him a pitcher of wine daily. Other lucrative administrative posts became his later.

1374? Chaucer began his unfinished work *The House of Fame*.

1382? Chaucer wrote *The Parlement of Fowles* – possibly for the marriage of Richard II.

1386 Like the Franklin in *The Canterbury Tales*, Chaucer was appointed 'Knight of the Shire' or Parliamentary representative for the county of Kent.

Early 1380s He wrote *Troilus and Criseyde*.

It seems that, in spite of the royal and noble patronage he enjoyed, Chaucer was an extravagant man, and money slipped through his fingers. In 1389 he was appointed Clerk of the King's Works by Richard II, but the position lasted only two years. Richard later gave him a pension of £20 for life, which Chaucer frequently asked for 'in advance'. Threats of arrest for non-payment of debts were warded off by letters of protection from the crown.

c. 1388 Chaucer probably began to formulate his ideas for *The Canterbury Tales* around this time.

1391 He was appointed deputy forester (an administrative post) in Petherton, Somerset, and may have spent some time there.

1399   Henry IV, son of John of Gaunt, became king, and Chaucer was awarded a new pension of 40 marks (about £26), which allowed him to live his few remaining months in comfort.

1400   Chaucer died in October, and was buried in Westminster Abbey.

CHAUCER THE WRITER AND SCHOLAR

Geoffrey Chaucer was actively involved in diplomatic life, moving in court circles, and travelling extensively; he was also an extremely well-read man. His writing shows the influence of classical authors, as well as more recent French and Italian works. The wide range of biblical, classical and contemporary literary references in the *The Canterbury Tales*, especially in the Wife of Bath's Prologue and Tale, bear witness to his learning, and he confesses to owning 60 books – a very considerable library in those days. Many of the ideas and themes which occur in *The Canterbury Tales* have been adapted from the works of classical and contemporary sources known to Chaucer and to at least some of his audiences. His earliest works, such as *The Book of the Duchess*, show the influence of courtly and and allegorical French love poetry, in particular the *Roman de la Rose*, a dream poem about the psychology of falling in love. *The Book of the Duchess* is a dream poem in this tradition.

The House of Fame, an unfinished narrative poem, shows influences from Chaucer's reading in Italian as well as French poetry. Chaucer is almost the only writer of the century outside Italy to show a knowledge of the *Divine Comedy* of Dante (1265–1321), but in this poem, he challenges Dante's claim that it is possible to know the truth about people's actions and motives in the past. Chaucer also admired the writings of two other Italians, Petrarch and Boccaccio; the latter's *Decameron* employs the linking device (in his case a group of sophisticated men and women, entertaining one another with story-telling in a country retreat, whilst the Black Death rages in Florence) that Chaucer was to use later with far greater subtlety, variety and skill.

In both *Troilus and Criseyde*, a re-telling of a tale of love and betrayal at the time of the Trojan War, and *The Canterbury Tales*, Chaucer shows the debt he owed to classical writers, in particular Ovid and Virgil. He was also familiar with the Bible and some of the writings of theologians highly respected in the Middle Ages, such St Jerome and St Augustine. He greatly admired the Roman philosopher Boethius, whose work *De Consolatione Philosophiae* (The Consolation of Philosophy) he translated from its original Latin into English. His writing shows an interest in astronomy and astrology, and he wrote one of the very first textbooks in English, *A Treatise on the Astrolabe*, explaining the working of this astronomical instrument for 'little Lewis', presumably a young son who died in infancy – we hear nothing of him later.

The social structure and Chaucer's satire

Society in Chaucer's time was more clearly structured than today. People's status was defined more closely, and the behaviour expected of them was more closely associated with their status. What we might now call classes were known as 'estates' in medieval times – groups of people within society, each of which had a function and rank. There were three estates: the lowest and largest consisted of ordinary people living ordinary lives and producing the food and services on which everyone depended; next came a smaller and richer group who were the defenders of society, the knights; and finally there was the clergy, whose function was to bind the whole society together with God. The function of each estate was to do the work allotted to it and in that way to live harmoniously with the other groups. Just as today we tend to judge people by their accent, their wealth or their job, so people were judged according to their estate in Chaucer's day. Since the idea was to search for a harmonious life on earth, reflecting the harmony of Heaven, there was a strong moral and spiritual overtone to the system: to perform one's estate function well was to do good, and to be 'worthy', a word used by Chaucer in many different ways. Life on earth, in theory at least, consisted of the exchange of services between estates, and anything that interfered with this exchange reduced human relationships, was displeasing to God, and destructive of good order.

Large systems that attempt to impose harmony on a whole society usually manage to do so only in theory, or in practice only to a limited extent or for limited periods of time. Attempts to live according to Marxism in Soviet Russia are perhaps a good example in our own time. Human frailty ensures that some people will make only a token effort to do what is expected of them; many people will not achieve much because they are weak or lazy; others will actively seek their own advantage without thought for the harm they do to others. Once the original system becomes diluted in this way, the old assumptions and rules are less compelling because they are less relevant in the new circumstances. New ideas, new functions and new aspirations attract people, and they gradually lose sight of the original ideal. Nevertheless, such systems can have a remarkable hold upon people's view of themselves; if they grow up within such a system of belief and practice, it will seem natural to them. They may be aware of their own shortcomings, and be surrounded by the evidence of other people's shortcomings, but they will cling to the idea of how they all ought to live. Ideas about how people ought to behave change slowly.

In The General Prologue we can see some of the changes happening. Characters such as the Knight or the Plowman pursue their vocations selflessly, fulfilling their functions in their different estates, but many other characters do not live in this way. Their world has become too complex for social and moral relationships to be expressed in this direct social manner. Many pressures for change arose during Chaucer's lifetime: the appalling mortality of the Black Death brought about great changes; the war with France flared up destructively and expensively from time to time; a new and vigorous commercial life developed after the Black Death; and religious authority was weakened when the Papacy itself was split for several decades during the fourteenth century, with rival popes in Rome and Avignon. These and many other factors were pushing the world into new attitudes and structures. Social or estate relationships were being replaced by relationships between individuals, with rank and function within society playing a lesser part. New functions were also arising – the Franklin's is an example – which owe little to the old world. He is a landowner but not technically one of the gentry, he is confident of his power, position and ideas, and feels able to shape his world much as he wishes.

Chaucer's audience would have known where each character belonged in the system, and how he or she ought to live and behave. Estates provided a moral and functional structure in which people could be placed, and an ideal against which to measure actual behaviour.

The gap between the ideal and the actual performance allows the possibility of satire. Satire is, broadly, the attempt to reform behaviour by making it more nearly approximate to the ideal, and to achieve this by making people and their actions ridiculous or laughable. An accepted ideal – or at least an accepted norm – is essential for effective satire; where behaviour is more or less a matter of opinion, disapproval of someone's behaviour is also no more than opinion. Chaucer, however, lived in an age when it was still possible to rely on some people's knowledge of estate structures, and he therefore presents his characters, usually without direct comment, leaving his audience to form a conclusion if they wish. Thus the Monk is shown as fond of hunting and good living; there is no direct criticism of him for not being quietly at work within his monastery, but it is still possible to question his way of living out his vows.

The solution to corruption is not usually a return to an ideal that has already proved impossible for many people. Estates satire was unlikely to bite very deep if it merely pointed the finger and said that things were better in the past. More promising would be a satire that saw corruption and recognised it, saw virtue and praised it, but also saw the real dilemmas faced by people of goodwill as the world changed around them.

Such is the estates satire of Chaucer. It is subtle. Corruption, such as the Pardoner's, that damages innocent and defenceless people, is shown as evil, the more so as it is part of an established official system. Cold corruption, such as the Summoner's, is shown as ugly and revolting. The Shipman's readiness to kill those whose ships he has overwhelmed in his piracy is mentioned with the offhand brevity with which he kills, but the skills and knowledge he needs to carry out his designs are also recognised. The Prioress's worldly vanities are dealt with more leniently by Chaucer, as her weakness affects only herself, and she does no intentional harm to others – though the potential for harm in a person of her position hovers in the background of Chaucer's description.

Discussion questions

1 What impression do you get of Chaucer 'the poet' and Chaucer 'the pilgrim' from The General Prologue?
2 List those pilgrims who are described mostly by their physical appearance. Why do you think this is so, and how do their descriptions differ from those of pilgrims whose moral and spiritual qualities are emphasised?
3 Chaucer lays great emphasis on ability and professionalism. Choose three characters where this is so, and consider the effect of such emphasis on Chaucer's readers.
4 What differences of tone or voice can you detect between the opening of The General Prologue and the account given of the early part of the pilgrimage, from line 717 onwards?
5 How would you describe the tension between worldly wealth and spiritual wealth in the descriptions of the pilgrims?

Glossary of frequently used words

al	entirely	hoom	home
al be	although	hoot	hot
als	as	ilke	this same
anon	immediately	kan	know, be able
array	dress, state	koude	knew how to
aventure	chance	morwe	morning
ay	always	nas	was not
been/ben	be	noght	not, nothing
bokeler	small round shield	noon	no, none
cleped	called	parfit	perfect
clerk	scholar, academic	person/persoun	parson
curteis	courteous, of gentle behaviour	solempne	dignified, impressive
		sondry	various
degree	social rank	swich	such
doon	do	than/thanne	then
eek	also	thries	thrice, three times
er	before	thriftily	efficiently
ese	pleasure	tweye	two
everich	every, each one	verray	true, real, exact
eyen	eyes	viage	journey
fer	far	wende	go
fredom	nobility, generosity	weren	were
fetisly	neatly, elegantly	whan that	when
gentil	noble, worthy	wight	person
goon	go	wood	mad
hem	them	woot	know
himselven	himself	yaf	gave
hir	their	ye	eye
hoole	whole	yeve/yeven	give
hire	her	yive	give

96